FEWER THINGS, BETTER

The courage to focus on
what matters most

More books by Angela Watson

Unshakeable:
20 Ways to Enjoy Teaching Every Day ... No Matter What

Awakened:
Change Your Mindset to Transform Your Teaching

The Awakened Devotional Study Guide
for Christian Educators

The Cornerstone:
Classroom Management That Makes Teaching
More Effective, Efficient, and Enjoyable

Fewer Things, Better:

The Courage to Focus on What Matters Most

Angela Watson

Due Season PRESS and Educational Services

For discounts on large quantities of this book for schools and other organizations, please email info@TheCornerstoneForTeachers.com.

Fewer Things, Better: The Courage to Focus on What Matters Most
by Angela Watson

Names and identifying details have been changed to protect the anonymity of persons and events mentioned herein.

Published by Due Season Press and Educational Services

ISBN-13: 978-0-9823127-4-2
ISBN-10: 0-98231

This book is dedicated to the innovative educators I've had the privilege of connecting with through the 40 Hour Teacher Workweek Club. Thank you for believing in my mission and having the courage to lead by example. Your daily work gives other teachers hope that there's a sustainable way to do an excellent job for kids and restore balance in an impossibly demanding profession.

This is our movement, and this book was inspired by what I've learned through coaching you and cheering you on in your journey. Your willingness to disrupt the status quo and challenge conventional beliefs about what it means to be a teacher is paving the way for others to step into their courage and power, too.

Participate in the Fewer Things Better Project

I've created a **free mini-course with printable workbook** to help you implement the ideas you're about to read. These resources will give you a clearer understanding of your priorities so you can develop an actionable plan for what "fewer things better" looks like in YOUR life.

I recommend reading the book first and then completing the exercises in the project, but take whatever approach feels right to you.

Go to **FTBproject.com** when you're ready to begin, and you can download all the resources.

Table of Contents

Belief #2: I set my own expectations in life and in teaching

Who said it has to be done that way?
Find more efficient and effective ways to meet the requirements
Brainstorm alternatives to school norms
3 ways to respond to school norms you dislike
Avoid being labeled "the angry teacher" by showing up with solutions
How privilege and reputation can be used to disrupt the status quo
Lead colleagues toward change and support those who speak up
Resist the "school family" manipulation
Dismantle the false "team player" obligations
Break the barrel instead of pulling each other down
Stop holding in resentment until you just burnout

Root out imposter syndrome
Recognize the value you bring to your work each day
Counter the feelings of not being or doing "enough"
Let go of "one right way" pressure and let your identity evolve
Allow other teachers to inspire you instead of comparing yourself
Self-reflect to find an approach in "the green zone"
Choose an accountability partner to help you grow your confidence

Redefine "normal" in a way that works for YOU
Notice how judgment keeps you from seeing new possibilities
How to figure out what you want more (and less of) in your life
Winners DO quit; they just quit the right things at the right time
Create boundaries, not ultimatums
When creating boundaries exacts too high a price
Accept the indignities of teaching for the love of the work

Belief #3: I know what's important and allocate time accordingly

What do you want your legacy to be?

How to build a legacy in your current season

Identify the daily habits that contribute to your legacy

You don't have to give the most time to your biggest priorities

5 steps to aligning daily life with your priorities

How to reduce time spent on low priorities to make time for higher ones

"I don't know how to prioritize" means "I'm not clear on what I want."

Plan, then execute — not both at the same time

Prioritize tasks with a list-making system

Use the 4-question test to help you eliminate tasks

Create a buffer day for life's little annoyances

Decide how to eliminate the tasks you repeatedly put off

Use small blocks of time with intentionality

Plan your lessons for a realistic (rather than ideal) day

Streamline elements of the school day that waste time

Eliminate good learning activities to make time for the best

"Kill your darlings" when everything doesn't fit

Resist the urge to reinvent the wheel and chase shiny objects

Belief #4: I ensure my needs are met to prevent overwhelm and exhaustion

Introduction

You CAN'T do it all
(and you don't have to try)

I'm guessing you've picked up this book because you want your life to have a real impact on the world. You care about making a difference, not only in the classroom, but in your family and community, too.

And yet that focus tends to feel impossible when you're always exhausted and overwhelmed.

How can you do what's meaningful when you're distracted by never-ending paperwork, meetings, errands, and housework?

How can you give the best of yourself when you're bogged down with mundane tasks and unfulfilling obligations?

This is the struggle I hear about constantly from countless teachers all over the world. So many educators want desperately to create better balance in their lives. But, there's always MORE to be done, and staying on top of everything feels like a losing battle.

Here's the truth these teachers hear far too rarely:

> *You are not to blame, and there's nothing wrong with YOU.*
>
> *The problem is that the job of teaching is extraordinarily demanding, and there's no clear path to managing all that's required (much less maintaining a personal life on top of work).*

Teaching requires an extremely complex skill set, and the stakes are high. With constant changes in technology, curriculum, standards, and leadership, it's rare that teachers have the opportunity to master one thing before being told they have to do things in a completely different way.

Compounding the issue is the emotional labor required in teaching. Our students come to us impacted by trauma and experiencing record levels of depression and anxiety. Helping kids overcome these obstacles is yet one more thing teachers are supposed to handle.

We find ourselves trying to pour from an empty cup, struggling to offer students true empathy, understanding, and support while feeling worn down and under-resourced ourselves.

Add to that the nearly impossible standards set by society for being a "good" teacher, spouse/partner, parent, etc., and the only reasonable conclusion is this:

Meeting all the expectations is impossible. You really CAN'T do everything that seemingly needs to be done.

So at some point, you have to give yourself permission to stop trying.

There's no magical productivity secret that will make it seem like there are 28 hours in a day. You can experiment endlessly with strategies for shifting tasks around and doing them more efficiently, and that still won't fix the root of the problem.

There are simply too many things demanding your time and attention.

The solution is NOT to manage your time better or work more efficiently. Or at least — that's not the place to start when you're overwhelmed.

The most important step is getting clarity: figuring out what matters most so you can do fewer things better.

You will always have more tasks than time, so you have to figure out what's most important and eliminate some things you feel you "have" to do. You must let go of the good to make time for the great.

Without this step, you'll feel like you're neglecting your health and your family because you work too much, and when you try to correct the balance at home, you'll feel like you're short-changing your students.

You'll be spreading yourself thin across so many areas that you won't do an effective job with ANY of them. A constant sense of guilt and overwhelm is almost unavoidable.

Throughout this book, you'll discover that *the things you say NO to are just as important as what you say YES to.*

This is the missing piece for many teachers who are reaching for the elusive goal of work/life balance. Very few of us give much thought to what we *don't* do.

Instead, we focus on doing as many things as possible, and pack our days with the maximum number of tasks we can handle. We look for ways to have more energy and time with the goal of getting more things done. Pushing ourselves to the limit is a daily practice. In fact, the day doesn't feel like a "success" unless we're collapsing into bed at night. Anything less than total exhaustion leaves us feeling uneasy, as if we could have made better use of our time.

We use "busy" as our barometer of success, and so we never stop to ask ourselves:

- *Am I filling my day with banal tasks and unfulfilling obligations because that's what everyone around me expects?*
- *Am I constantly trying to be more efficient with tasks that I shouldn't be doing at all?*
- *How can I create time for the most important things instead of trying to do as many things as possible?*

These are some of the questions I'll help you answer through this book. I'll teach you the process of freeing up time, attention, and energy for the things that really matter: the activities that truly impact student learning; the practices that make you a more effective educator; the routines that make your home and personal life more fulfilling.

It's time to release yourself from that feeling of never having done enough.

It's time to stop giving in to the pressure to be constantly busy.

It's time to prioritize tasks that really matter, and truly let go of the rest.

It's time to do fewer things, so what remains can be done even better.

We'll tackle this process through some actionable strategies for reducing your workload, but you won't find a simple checklist of things to eliminate.

Most of the work involves shifting your mindset and changing your perspective so you can create healthier habits.

You see, doing fewer things better, is a lot like getting in shape physically. It's fairly easy to understand the practical measures which will help you achieve your goal.

And yet if keeping off extra pounds was as simple as eliminating or cutting back on certain foods, wouldn't everyone be at their ideal weight? If the solution to work/life balance was as simple as not bringing work home, wouldn't all teachers have enough downtime to relax?

Getting a clear idea of WHAT to do is the easier part.

Figuring out HOW to follow through on a daily basis is much more complicated.

That's because there are school, societal, and cultural norms which impact our choices about how time should be spent. These outside expectations shape the standards we set for ourselves and muddle our beliefs about what's important.

We also experience a wide variety of emotions which pull us away from making rational choices. That's part of the experience of being human: we have excuses, exceptions, self-imposed rules, and limiting beliefs that keep us from doing what's best for ourselves.

These are some of the barriers we're going to break through in this book so that you can truly *give yourself permission* to do fewer things better, and feel confident about your choices.

We'll also examine systemic issues, bureaucratic restraints, inefficient instructional practices, and everything else that creates a disconnect between what you *want* your life as a teacher to be like, and what it's actually like.

The goal here is clarity and focus — to release anything that's not serving you well, so you can open yourself up to a new approach in the way you spend your time.

TOGETHER, WE'LL CHALLENGE THE CORRELATION BETWEEN HOURS WORKED AND EFFECTIVENESS. IT'S NOT ABOUT HOW MUCH YOU'RE WORKING; IT'S WHAT YOU'RE FOCUSING ON IN THOSE HOURS.

As you read, you'll gain clarity on what's most important in every aspect of your life and work so you can allocate time to your biggest priorities. You'll deepen the courage it takes to live with intentionality, so you can do more of what you love and let go of habits and expectations that are holding you back.

The end result will look different for each teacher. So rather than tell you what to do with your time and what not to, I'll simply guide you down the path by instilling four core beliefs. These will help you discover the answers for yourself.

Let's get started.

Part One

I AM WORTHY OF BETTER AND CHANGE IS POSSIBLE FOR ME RIGHT NOW

"*The root cause of burnout is not that we have too much to do. It's the feeling that the things we do aren't meaningful or don't reflect who we really are.*"
— Dr. Ayala Malach Pines

If a teacher's to-do list was centered on engaging with kids and helping them learn, most of us wouldn't mind a long, busy, or even hectic day. There would be an immense satisfaction that comes from knowing you made a difference and had meaningful interactions with kids.

Teacher burnout stems largely from the disconnect between the most fulfilling part of the work and how the majority of your time is spent.

So much of your energy is focused on paperwork, email, compiling and analyzing data, attending meetings, and other non-instructional tasks that the *actual work of teaching children* is no longer the primary focus.

Many teachers not only have limited opportunities to be creative and connect with students, but rarely have the energy to do those things well because they're so exhausted from handling everything else.

When you begin to view your work through the lens of doing fewer things better, you give yourself permission to clear away obligations that aren't meaningful, both at school and in your personal life. You learn to continually identify things that drain your energy, and streamline, automate, delegate, or eliminate them whenever possible.

The goal is to spend the majority of your time doing things which are fulfilling and impactful. That holds for your instructional time, work hours before and after school, and personal time.

This process is about mindfulness and intentionality. It's about viewing your time as a series of choices, and stepping into your power to exercise autonomy whenever possible.

If you notice feelings of skepticism as you consider this, that's perfectly normal. In fact, skepticism might be your natural reaction anytime you read productivity advice or hear teachers talk about having better work/life balance:

Must be nice for them, but it wouldn't work for me. My situation is different, and there's nothing I can do about it.

If that's how you're feeling, this first core belief we'll explore together can be the game-changer:

YOU MUST BE WILLING TO BELIEVE THAT CHANGE IS POSSIBLE FOR YOU, AND THAT YOU ARE WORTHY OF HAVING A MORE FULFILLING, BALANCED LIFE.

You cannot write this off as feel-good mumbo jumbo. You cannot just agree in theory or wish this was true.

You need to actually believe it — to know it to be true, to feel it deep in your bones — so that it guides all your decision-making about how you spend your time.

Too often, we try to take action without shifting our beliefs. We look for quick hacks or tricks that make life easier and less stressful. But if you want to permanently change your actions (the choices you make about what to do), you'll be far more successful if you change your identity (the way you see yourself).

When you truly believe that you have options and deserve to have a more fulfilling life, the clarity you want becomes possible. You'll be clear on when to say no, and have the courage you need to confidently do less when everyone else is trying to do more.

Together, you and I are going to shift paradigms and examine the stories you're telling yourself, so you can learn to see yourself and your life choices in a different way.

Self-reflection is the most important part of this work, because once you know *how to think* in a productive, healthy, balanced way, then living out your beliefs through your daily choices becomes much easier.

1

Recognizing the true potential of your time

I was an elementary teacher for 11 years before becoming an instructional coach. And like most teachers, I had a substantial amount of materials I'd drag to and from school on a regular basis: treats for a class party, containers I'd found at Target, materials for science experiments, and tons of papers to grade.

I had, of course, purchased that quintessential teacher item: the collapsible rolling cart. It's sometimes known as "the cart of shame" because of the feelings it induces when you roll that same cart back to school the next day with all the paperwork untouched.

My cart of shame collapsed after a few years of heavy use, and I needed a replacement badly. I ran a quick search on Amazon, and sure enough, they had the cart in stock.

Unfortunately, it was $34.99, which seemed a bit steep. Surely I could find it cheaper.

So, I spent some time combing through the listings on eBay. *Aha!* I found an auction beginning at 99 cents. I placed my bid. Now all I had to do was wait a week for the auction to end (although I spent that week checking it obsessively to see if I'd been outbid).

I lost.

I decided to turn to an online group of teachers who sold used materials.

I searched through the listings there, but didn't see any rolling carts currently for sale. When I asked, a couple people made suggestions, but nothing ever panned out.

I continued to comparison shop online, and eventually discovered a teacher store about a half hour away which had the cart on sale.

Finally! My perfect rolling cart, and it was only $29.99!

At last I could check this item off my to-do list, feeling 100% confident I had achieved my goal of purchasing the cart for the lowest possible price.

As I got in my car to drive to the store, I paused.

A thought suddenly struck me:

I had tackled this task repeatedly over a two-week time period, spending around two hours hunting for the cart, and now I was about to drive 30 minutes out of my way (and 30 minutes back home) in order to save myself … a whopping five bucks.

> *I was incredibly intentional about that five dollars, but never even thought to count the cost of my time.*

I had traded hours of my time (a finite resource, which can never be recovered) to preserve the tiniest bit of money (which is infinite, because more can always be earned or received).

Time can be budgeted and invested instead of just spent

Maybe you're thinking, *Wait, Angela. My money definitely feels just as limited as my time.*

And yet regardless of what happens in the future, it's a pretty solid bet that more opportunities to get money will be possible for you. Another pay check will come in a few weeks, and then another after that. If not, other options for getting more money are available.

Your time, on the other hand, is permanently running out. Each day, you have less time to be alive, and you can't ever get more, no matter how hard you work.

Despite this fact, I'm guessing you're like me in that story. You, too, are watching your money much more closely than you're watching your time.

Even if you're not strict about budgeting, you know the price of everything you buy. You count the cost before making financial commitments. You mentally weigh your options before taking the plunge to buy something that's not absolutely necessary.

That's a good thing — but it's not enough, because money isn't the most valuable asset we have. You can always make more money. You can never make more time.

 IMAGINE HOW OUR LIVES WOULD BE DIFFERENT IF WE GAVE OUR TIME THE SAME LEVEL OF THOUGHT AND CONSIDERATION AS OUR MONEY.

It's common sense to create a financial budget so you know where your money is going and can make sure you have enough allocated for everything that's important. But have you ever created a budget for your *time*?

Have you ever mapped out the hours you're willing to allocate to various aspects of life to ensure time is spent on what's most important?

If you're like most people, the answer is no. Most of us simply wake up each day and try to cram in as many things as possible. Whatever is most urgent is where our time and attention goes. The things which are top priority in theory (such as a relationship with a partner or taking care of our bodies) get whatever time is leftover, which is never very much.

Don't beat yourself up about this. You probably weren't taught to think about your time in this way, and have never been given a simple method for doing it. (I'll help you create this "budget" later, so you can make sure you're investing time into what really matters.)

Plan to make time, not hope to find time

When we take money more seriously than time, we tend to fritter time away and lose track of where it was spent. Living the "fewer things better" way means that you invest your time the same way you'd like to invest your money.

You can spend your time and money on things that are gone quickly, or invest them in things that will pay you back dividends later on.

The time you've put into reading this book wasn't spent. It's not gone now — it was *invested*. For each hour you invest in reading how to simplify your life, you will get back dividends later on: more time, focus, balance, and clarity.

People who manage their money well tend to make choices with the long-term plan in mind. They don't just buy whatever feels good or urgent in the moment. They know that means they won't be able to pay their bills, save up for a vacation or repairs, or have enough money for other things that are important to them.

People who manage their time well do the same. They don't just do whatever feels good or urgent in the moment, if they know that means they'll run out of time for other things they really need or want.

When we don't have a plan for our time or money, those things slip away from us very quickly, and we don't even realize it.

"Didn't I just get paid? Where did the whole paycheck go already?" isn't much different from *"Wasn't it just 8 pm? How is it midnight already?"*

When you need more money, you don't just hope for it, or try to "find it" someplace. The most reliable way to get more money is to look for ways to make more of it.

So, don't try to find time; *make* time for the things that matter.

Do you REALLY value your own time (and insist others do, too)?

I hope you're nodding along, believing that time deserves as much (or more) consideration as money, and agreeing that it's important to make conscious choices about spending it.

But let's make this personal. It's YOUR time that's valuable, not just time in general.

And you deserve to take control of how your time is used.

Often, it's challenging to live out this principle because thoughts like these swirl in the back of our minds:

- *I'm afraid people won't like me or won't think I'm a team player if I protect my time.*
- *I don't like conflict, and it's uncomfortable for me to set boundaries.*

- *The things I'm doing help others: I don't want to let them down by saying no.*

Many teachers can relate to these feelings, and it's an important reason why we have trouble taking charge of how we use our time.

I want you to believe with your whole heart — not just agree with, but internalize and live by — the belief that *your wants and needs matter just as much as everyone else's.*

You are no more important and no less important than every other person.

Therefore, your goals and priorities deserve consideration. You deserve to have time for things that matter to you and which help you maintain your mental, emotional, physical, and spiritual health.

The courage to define your time for yourself

You deserve a life that is lived with intention, and that's designed around what matters to you.

You deserve a life where your own needs are met instead of having them constantly pushed to the side to meet everyone else's expectations.

You deserve to be able to show up for yourself, your family, your friends, and your school each day feeling rested and content.

You deserve a life that is not rushed and hectic and stressful. It is possible to live a modern 21st century existence and still have space to breathe, reflect, and think.

It's not easy to get there, but this is a journey that's worth undertaking. The years are going to pass, anyway. You can either rush through them at a harried pace, or you can spend them getting to know who you are (and what you want out of life) so your time can be used accordingly.

And the more you practice this, the more intuitive the process will become.

In the beginning, saying *no* when everyone else says *yes* will take a lot of courage. Creating boundaries around your time will take courage, too.

That courage can be found by getting clarity on what really matters. When you know your core values and the purpose of your life, it becomes much easier to be decisive and unapologetic about your choices.

You'll no longer be willing to waste your time — and therefore waste your life — on things that don't matter.

When you believe that you deserve better, you stop settling for the status quo. You start to see new possibilities, and you realize that change is possible for YOU.

Never give away your power by insisting you don't have any control over your time. Change IS possible for you, and it's possible right now.

You can choose to let go of expectations (from others, and from within yourself) to focus more on things you care about.

Your beliefs about time will teach people how to treat you

As you begin to respect yourself and your time as much as you respect your money, the way you interact with other people will change.

You'll no longer assume that when someone asks you to do something, you must at least *try* to fit in the request.

All those small tasks add up, and you'll mentally weigh the cost of taking on another obligation instead of defaulting to "yes" because the person made it seem like no big deal. You're the only one who truly understands your current obligations, energy level, and so on — and you will make the decisions about what you can handle instead of letting others decide for you.

You will begin to make time for your own needs and balance them with the things others need from you. Your sense of purpose and vision for how you want to spend your time will give you confidence to prioritize your goals.

And I think you'll be amazed at how others respond.

There are so few people who are truly intentional about their time that the people who ARE tend to garner tremendous respect. Having the ability to evaluate priorities thoughtfully and say "no" when needed is almost like a superpower in an overcommitted world.

People may not *like* that you're less available to cater to their every whim, but they will learn to *respect* you and the way you set boundaries. You will grow to prefer being respected, rather than needing to be liked.

Other people will stop viewing you as their go-to person for every request, and will begin to ASK rather than TELL you what they need.

They will stop depending on you to pick up all the slack, and take more initiative themselves (or ask other people to handle their share, too).

When you confidently demonstrate to others that you value your own time, you will find yourself experiencing a new freedom that you never thought was possible.

You'll realize that you have the power to question the status quo and let go of expectations that aren't working for you.

Question the "normal" way to use time

This kind of intentionality and self-confidence will require you to think outside the box, because it will contradict the way you see most people around you using their time. It's normal in our society to feel exhausted, overwhelmed, and pulled in a million directions.

Whether or not we admit it publicly, most of us feel like we're going on a wing and prayer every day. That's the natural impact of a frantic pace and constantly plugged-in world most people choose to participate in.

If you approach time in the "normal" way — the way most people in our society do it — you will get normal results. Normal means never having a moment to breathe, and talking about your next vacation on the first day back from the last one.

Normal is not synonymous with healthy. Normal will probably not give you the results you want.

If you sign up for every activity and social obligation that other families in your community participate in, then you, too, will find your evenings and weekends stretched to the max.

If you model your teaching approach after colleagues who work 70 hour weeks, then you, too, will work long hours.

If you follow the mindless *work-housework-dinner-TV-bed* routine that many people fall into, then you, too, will feel like you're stuck on a hamster wheel with no time for the things you care about.

This sounds obvious when we stop to think about it, but who makes time to stop and think about it? If you want to do fewer things better, begin by questioning the "normal" way to spend time.

Examine the pressure you feel to fit in or do things like everyone else. Bring your awareness to school, cultural, and societal expectations. Then you can decide which standards are serving you well, and which you want to release yourself from.

2

Understanding why it's hard for teachers to say no

Our individual mindsets and habits are not created in a bubble. We've all been influenced by outside expectations which have shaped our beliefs about how our time should be spent and what it means to be a teacher.

So, if we want to question what we've come to see as "normal", we have to consider the structures and systems which brought us to this point.

In the early days of what's now evolved into our public school system in the United States, women teachers were required to be single and childless. They didn't have to juggle work/life balance because the expectation was that they wouldn't have much of a personal life apart from teaching. The profession was seen by many as a calling which one should whole-heartedly devote one's life to (much like a nun).

According to Dana Goldstein's book *The Teacher Wars*, another prevailing belief by the early 1800s was that teaching was an extension of mothering. It was seen by many as unskilled labor which focused mostly on imparting morality rather than intellectual skills or academics. As you would expect for a profession that was viewed this way, paltry wages were the norm.

Salaries were lowest for women teachers, since they had few other options at the time and their labor was seen as less valuable than men's. Goldstein points out the advantage of this for state governments, who purposefully hired a majority-female workforce because it was cheaper. Male teachers were compensated at double the rate of female teachers, though their wages were still less than what they could earn in many other professions available to them.

It's clear that the teaching profession in America was never designed to offer a lifetime of strong wages or a sustainable workload. Our schools have a 200+ year history of undervaluing the necessary skill sets of a good educator, offering low compensation, and making all-consuming demands on teachers' personal lives due to the perception of the work as a "calling" which they should gladly sacrifice for.

No matter how much has changed in recent decades, these core problems are still the same. The modern expectation that teachers be degreed and highly trained has not come with competitive pay scales. It hasn't shifted public opinion of teaching as glorified babysitting which anyone can do. And, the assumption of selfless devotion to students at the expense of one's own needs still persists.

Local governments slash school budgets year after year while raising the bar for teachers to a nearly impossible level. With each new generation of educators, the demands are pressed to greater extremes.

It almost seems like a test: *How much, exactly, can we force teachers to give, and how little can we get away with giving them in return?*

Lawmakers know if the school doesn't provide what kids need to thrive, we as educators will pick up the slack. We will figure out a way to get kids what they need and work countless unpaid hours to do it. We'll be the only group of professionals routinely making supplies from scratch and spending our own money to get the job done.

It's been this way for so long that we've internalized the expectation. We believe it's just what good teachers do: *Give selflessly of your time, energy, and meager paycheck for the sake of the children.*

A former teacher named Seth Nichols observed this phenomenon as a man in our profession (which is still majority — 77% — women.) He posits that the damaging norms in education persist because the folks in charge take advantage of what Seth calls, "The Women's Honor Code: Do whatever it takes for the kids, at any cost."

What follows is an adapted excerpt from a blog post written by Seth one month before he left the teaching profession. (Thank you, Seth, for allowing me to share your words here.)

Women's Honor Code: Do it for the kids, no matter the cost

❝ *Women are done being taken advantage of. It's not just about pay. It's about respect. It's about boundaries crossed and people used. It's about unrealistic, unspoken expectations systemically enforced, leaving the perceived inability to speak up for oneself.*

It's about a mass of subservient people waking up one day to see the reality of what they've been putting up with all along.

When you hear stories and shine light into cultural blind spots, you start to see that there have been wide scale, nationally-accepted inequalities kept alive for decades in the dungeons of school halls, among the nation's largest female workforce.

I was in a data analysis meeting with my female colleagues, needing student whiteboards for math. As a norm, I don't request purchases from the "company." I often forget it's even an option. When I mentioned it to a co-teacher on the way to the meeting, she gave me a sarcastic, "Good LUCK ..."

I said, "Hey, if this school, on its $10 million budget, can't afford $50 whiteboards — how do they expect someone supporting a family of 6 on a teacher's salary to be able to?" She said she had never thought of that.

She had never thought of that. This is our culture. Where you aren't allowed to think about asking for your needs to be met.

The given is to figure it out. Because women will. Had I asked 20 different teachers about whiteboards, 10 of them would start spewing out names of stores. The other 10 would give me some DIY weekend instructions that involve table saws. Seldom would any of them think to say, "Umm, ask for them ..."

Injustice and oppression thrive in places where the norms are never questioned.

The fact that the whiteboards were such a small purchase actually illuminates the problem. A man's operative norm tends to be, "Since it's not a big deal, the company should have no problem helping you out."

A woman's tends to be, "Since it's not a big deal, you should be able to handle it yourself."

Nothing we handle is a huge deal. But the sum total of all of the straws on the camel's back have become a crushing weight for so many.

It's not about the pay. It's about all of the ways an entire sector of the country's most selfless givers have been complicit to a system that has evolved to bilk them every way it can: of their time, their money, their energy, and their emotions.

Pay for it yourself.

Create it yourself.

Stay late and put on that function yourself.

Meet during your time.

Work during your weekend.

Be kind to people yelling, ignoring, cursing, and hitting you.

Then, make sure they pass the new standards.

And be prepared to take bullets for them, too.

These things are not said as much as they are collectively understood, much worse. Tacit expectations are the ones we feel least able to challenge.

See, behind each one of these expectations lies the unspoken threat — "Don't you love your kids?"

I've learned that a woman will do almost anything to prove she's a good caretaker and nurturer. The female honor code is, do it for the kids, no matter the cost. Don't ask questions or be perceived as disloyal to your children.

And, while each woman should be responsible for enforcing her own boundaries, we should not be systematically violating them, either.

I want the women of my world free to be fiercely loyal mothers and selfless givers, without some manipulative loser-of-a-school system taking advantage of her selflessness …

The system, in many places, bears a creepy resemblance to an abusive husband. If she loses "him" [her job], she feels like she would lose everything.

He constantly tells her she's not good enough, and has spreadsheets with scores to prove it.

He blames her for the kids' problems, and offers no real help in fixing them. But she stays and puts up with him — because she loves the kids.

He is boxing her in, manipulating her, and implicitly calling her loyalty into question every time she doesn't bend over backwards to appease him and make him look good.

Should we be surprised that she's finally walking out? 𝄐

Reject the idea that working harder will prove your value

So much of a female educator's workload — as a teacher, wife, or mom — is undervalued, and either unpaid or underpaid.

And no matter your gender, you've likely had a lifetime of people undermining your work with off-handed comments such as, "How cute, you get to play with kids all day" and "Must be nice to have summers off" and "I couldn't get a job in my field so I figured I'd just teach for a year or two while I look for something better."

These remarks are obviously frustrating, but they're not innocuous. When you hear demeaning comments enough times from enough different people, you can't help but internalize them a bit.

The constant undervaluing of our work is a driving force behind the pressure to always do more.

It leaves us feeling continual pressure to prove ourselves and the value of our contributions. On some level, we believe that if we have enough productive accomplishments, then society as a whole will finally appreciate us, compensate us fairly, and show us respect.

So, we share memes on social media about buying school supplies out of pocket, not being able to take a bathroom break, and working on our summer "vacation" to let non-educator friends know just how demanding the profession really is.

We're frustrated that no one understands the demands of teaching unless they've lived it, and that manifests in a constant desire to prove it to people anyway, and thereby prove our worth to the taxpayers who remind us they fund our salaries.

When that insecurity drives the way we spend our time, the outcome is almost always troubling. We feel like we must say yes to everything that's asked, because we see it as necessary evidence of our dedication and effectiveness.

But the more things we demonstrate we can handle, the more things get piled on our plates. In the end, we're just wearing ourselves out and giving ourselves more things to feel resentful about, because the demands for unpaid labor never end.

Release yourself from the martyr mentality

The pressure on teachers to sacrifice endlessly creates a culture in which we are desperately trying to show that *we do the most*.

It's like a competition for martyrdom, and it's ingrained in us from the first days of our teacher training programs. We are told repeatedly — by everyone around us — that we will never make a lot of money in this profession, while also being told that teaching is the most important profession in the world.

> We are groomed from the start to accept that we will always be undervalued and underpaid, and the tacit implication is that we must be okay with that sacrifice if we really care about kids. In fact, the more okay with it you are and the more you are willing to sacrifice, the more people will consider you a dedicated, effective teacher.

A pre-service educator recently shared, "I feel compelled to tell people that I want to teach in a Title I school because I'm afraid they'll think I'm not in teaching for the right reasons if I'm not working with the kids who supposedly need me the most."

Another teacher told me, "I work in a private school in a well-to-do neighborhood, and I constantly feel guilty about it. I'm afraid people think I'm lazy for wanting the 'easy' teaching job."

An "easy" teaching job. Can you imagine?

And yet, these are the subconscious beliefs that comprise our collective teaching identity:

- *The harder the teaching job, the more it proves I care about kids.*
- *The more I pile onto my plate, the more dedicated I am.*
- *The worse the working conditions I endure, the tougher I am and the more worthy of respect I am.*

These are the beliefs which make the "savior complex" such a common problem amongst teachers. We think we're there to save the kids from their dangerous communities or negligent parents who "don't care."

We develop a deficit lens in which we focus only on the limitations and lack amongst those we serve. We pressure ourselves to do whatever it takes to "rescue" kids.

We are conditioned to see ourselves as the hero of kids' stories instead of seeing kids as the heroes of their own stories.

Not only will a savior complex harm your students, but it will also wear you out.

It's impossible to create better balance when you feel responsible for saving children and need to constantly prove how much you're doing to help them.

A savior or hero's entire identity is wrapped up in saving the victims, and nothing else matters — it must get done at any physical, emotional, or financial cost.

A supporter takes responsibility only for the factors within their control. A supporter derives a sense of self-worth from their inherent value which is not measured by how hard they work. Therefore, a supporter has nothing to prove to themselves or others.

Change your identity of being overworked & underappreciated

You can change your identity from savior to supporter, and withdraw from the contest for Most Dedicated Teacher in the Most Difficult Teaching Job Ever.

In fact, that's the critical piece of this transformation. If you think that taking the toughest teaching job and working endless hours is necessary to prove you care, any improvement in your workload will always be impossible.

Cutting back on anything will make you feel less dedicated to kids, and you will constantly compare yourself to other teachers who sacrifice more.

After all, if we left school at 3 p.m., we'd lose our "street cred" to the teachers who stayed until dinnertime, and the principal might think we're doing the bare minimum. Saying no to an extracurricular would mean our plates are less full than the colleagues who said yes, which means others might view us as lazy and not in the profession for "the right reasons."

This same mindset plays out in our personal lives, too (particularly for women, because of the conditioning that our value is reflected in how clean, attractive, and well-managed our homes are).

If we stepped back on household duties and didn't appear frazzled and tired, our family and friends might not recognize how much we do behind the scenes and will respect us less as moms, wives, or whatever else our identity is tied to.

Being overworked, underpaid, and unappreciated — yet continuing to give 110% every day — is part of our collective identity as educators. And we are all hardwired to reject changes that don't fit with our identities.

You won't be able to follow through on steps to reduce your workload until that no longer conflicts with your identity as someone who must do *anything* for the kids and be hard at work every minute to prove your worth.

Challenge the correlation between hours worked and effectiveness

The reason I understand self-sabotaging identities so well is because of my personal struggles with them.

I used to be that teacher who reveled in outsiders' admiration of my bravery and dedication, because announcing the neighborhood I taught in was the only time I ever felt my work was respected.

I used to be that teacher who would sit in professional development and listen primarily for ideas that *wouldn't* work, and then "what about" the presenter so she knew how challenging my class was to teach and how hard it was to be in the classroom.

I used to be that teacher who would purposefully take on unnecessary projects, and then complain endlessly about how overworked I was.

You get the picture. And it wasn't until I hit a point of major burnout that I realized change would have to start with how I viewed myself.

Maybe it's time for you to ask some of the questions I had to grapple with, too:

- *Do I want people to agree that I have a terribly hard job with completely unreasonable demands, or do I want to enjoy my work?*

- *Do I want the satisfaction that comes from seeing myself as a martyr, or do I want to figure out what my needs are and make sure they're met?*
- *Do I want to win the Hardest Job in the World award, or do I want to live a fulfilling, well-balanced life?*

You have to get real about what you want, and decide if you're actually motivated to change.

Because sometimes we don't want things to improve. We just want to wallow. We want to talk about how awful and difficult things are, and have others commiserate and admire us for all the hardship we manage to endure.

I've been there. And it's okay for you to be there, too. Just don't stay stuck there.

At any point in time, you can decide to stop repeating to yourself how exhausting everything is and let go of excuses for why your life could never be any different.

You can stop measuring your worth by what other people think of you and how much you do for others. You can disassociate the number of hours you work with your perception of effectiveness and dedication.

When you shift those beliefs, you create space to be intentional about how you use your unpaid time. You can begin to focus more on what matters instead of trying to keep up with what everyone else appears to be doing.

It is a myth that every teacher has to work endless unpaid hours to do a great job for kids. The truth is that working more hours does not equate with more effectiveness. It's what you do with the hours that makes a difference.

3

Examining your stories about what "has to" be done

The way that you see yourself and the stories you tell about how your time "must be" used will always limit your possibilities, until you examine those stories, decide which ones serve you, and toss out the ones that don't.

I can give you lots of strategies for streamlining, but if your story is that a productive day means working until you don't have an ounce of energy left, how can you buy into the concept of doing fewer things better?

I can share easy ways to reduce your workload, but if your story is that things "have to be done" the way you're currently doing them, how will you have the courage to disrupt the status quo?

The stories we tell ourselves may seem irrefutable, but don't always hold up under examination.

The story is not the facts. The story is what we make the facts mean. The story is our interpretation of the facts and the conclusion we jump to.

Before you can get into changing the facts — the actual workload and the demands on your time — you need strategies for distinguishing between the facts and the stories you tell yourself about the facts.

Let's unpack some of these stories that create an unhealthy identity, so you can begin to see yourself and your work in a new way.

If it's a priority, we find the time; if not, we find an excuse

One story that a lot of teachers tell themselves is this: *"School consumes all of my time so I can't do anything else."*

But is that really true?

Let's break this down and examine the facts without the *story* about the facts.

There are 168 hours in a week. Let's say you're contracted to work around 40 hours, and you work another 20 hours every week for free.

That's 60 hours a week spent on school-related tasks, leaving you with 108 hours to do everything else. If you factor in around 7 hours of sleep a night, that still leaves you with 59-60 hours a week for yourself, family, and household tasks.

60 hours a week in which you're not working or sleeping is a pretty significant amount of time to accomplish things and enjoy your life.

It's simply not true that all you have time for is work. Your work hours and your "free" hours are exactly the same: 60 each. And, 20 of your work hours are not contractually required or scheduled!

The story that you have no time for anything but work doesn't have to be your reality. When you can let go of that story, you open yourself up to seeing the facts more clearly. The truth isn't that school consumes every moment of time.

The truth is that most of your "free time" doesn't really *feel* "free." Most of it is not being spent on things that are meaningful and enjoyable.

Your evenings and weekends fly by with errands and appointments and commuting and household drudgery. You're trying to recuperate from work while also rushing from one activity to the next, with few opportunities to connect deeply to what matters most.

Enter the principle of "fewer things better."

We have to let go of the fantasy that we can keep all our current commitments and still find excess time and energy to pour into the things we love.

That might happen occasionally. But occasionally is not enough to move you toward your long term goals or have enough quality time for the people and activities you care about.

If you know that something is going to be worth the investment of time — be it exercising, eating dinner as a family, or reading a book like this one — you have to make time for it. You can get benefits from any of those activities if you're spending just one hour of a 168-hour week on them.

Everyone can find one hour in their week (and most can find an hour in their day) that is being squandered on things which are unnecessary, unfulfilling, or inefficient.

The people who accomplish their goals and live the life they want don't naturally have more time. In fact, no one has enough time for the things they care about. But you can *make* time.

You can decide which obligations are less important and reduce the time allocated to those things, in order to do more of what you want.

Differentiate between work as a hobby and true work

Most people in education don't think of their jobs as something they do for a set number of hours each day and then forget completely about. Teaching is who you ARE (or more accurately, a part of who you are).

Maybe you spend your weekends searching flea markets for cool artifacts you could bring into your classroom. Or, you watch documentaries at home and record them to play clips for your students. You might read books to improve your teaching craft or collaborate with other educators online.

Work/life balance makes it sound like you have to separate the work part of yourself from the life part of yourself, when for many teachers, the two cannot be easily separated … and you may not even want to try.

I became a teacher because I was truly passionate about the work. I enjoy finding and sharing ideas. I love creating elaborate activities and curriculum materials. It's fun for me to dream up different ways of decorating and organizing the learning environment.

When I was in the classroom, those were a few aspects of teaching that I gladly pursued in my free time. That work was like a hobby, or even a passion. I worked on those things far beyond the extent required or expected. I didn't *want* to limit the time I spent on them.

Grading papers, on the other hand? That was real, required work. So was entering data, documenting interventions, returning parent phone calls, and responding to emails. Those were not activities I wanted to spend my evenings and weekends completing.

It's important to distinguish between "hobby work" and "real work," because that will ease any resentment you (or your loved ones) feel about your habit of "working all the time."

Perhaps your 65 hour weeks are more like 50 hour weeks when you consider the time spent on "hobby work" such as Twitter chats, attending students' extracurricular activities, making gifts for coworkers, decorating for special events, and so on.

Some of those examples sound awful to me, by the way — they'd definitely be considered real work because I'd only do them if required. But I know teachers who enjoy all of those activities. The delineation between hobby work and real work is quite personal.

The guiding principle is this:

 IF YOU'RE ENJOYING THE WORK AND GOING BEYOND WHAT'S EXPECTED BY CHOICE, IT'S NOT REALLY WORK. IT'S SOMETHING YOU'RE *CHOOSING* TO DO BECAUSE YOU LIKE DOING IT AND IT'S MEANINGFUL.

Once you distinguish between real work and hobby work, you can either cut back on some of the hobby work in order to focus on something else, or you can embrace it wholeheartedly.

The only path that *isn't* viable is continuing to do hobby work incessantly while feeling resentful and complaining that you have no life apart from school. You have total control of those activities, and you are responsible for considering the trade-offs you're making.

Debunk the myth that you can't take anything off your plate

There's one story that I would love to eliminate for every person who reads this book: *"I don't have a choice; I have to."*

This is the catch-all story we tell ourselves about any obligation which has no obvious recourse.

And yet, here's the truth.

If you're the person making dinner every night; if you're constantly chauffeuring your children around to various activities; if you're the one running all the photocopies for your colleagues; if you're spending all your weekends grading papers; if you're responding to work emails every night at 10 o'clock ... these things are *all your choice.*

Think about it — the way you spend your time may not be an intentional choice you are deliberately making, and there might not be a lot of good alternatives.

But there is no law of the universe that mandates any of these things. They're not written into your job contract or marriage vows. There are plenty of teachers who don't do these things — probably even teachers at your own school with the same administrative requirements and a similar workload.

To some extent, every habit you have is a choice. The question is whether you are willing to live with the consequences of making a different choice. You could stop any of those habits, if you were willing to live with the results.

For example, you could stop making dinner, and let your family members fend for themselves. If you choose not to, it's because there's some reason you feel it's worthwhile to make dinner every night.

Maybe you want to make sure everyone's eating healthy meals. Maybe you don't feel like trying to coax your partner into cooking more, or you don't want to eat the meals they select. Maybe you just don't want anyone in "your" kitchen messing things up!

If you stop to think about WHY you're choosing to hold yourself responsible for dinner prep every night, you might realize there isn't a reason that's important enough to justify the personal cost, and start considering alternatives.

Choosing to see cooking every night as a choice will allow you to think about more possibilities. For example: taking turns with others in your household, meal exchanges with friends, picking up food from a restaurant on the way home from work, batching your meal prep so you can quickly reheat food later in the week, or eating simple meals like cereal or sandwiches.

These are just a few of the choices you *could* make. Some of them would have consequences you don't really like, such as costing more money, or allowing for less variety in your meals. Those repercussions are why you continue to choose cooking every night.

But make no mistake: it is a choice, so own that choice. Don't complain about it constantly and bemoan the fact that you spend hours on meal planning and prep. You are choosing to take on that responsibility in that way.

Reframe obligations so that how you spend your time is a choice

Try answering the questions below for an obligation you are resentful about doing but feel is not a choice.

This exercise will help you figure out why you continue to go along with that choice, so that you can either make peace with it or find alternatives that are worth the trade-off. (There's a free printable chart for this exercise available at FTBproject.com.)

1) What is the thing I dislike and why do I feel like it's not a choice?
2) What are some alternative choices I could make (even if I don't like the consequences)?
3) Why have I not made one of these other choices? What benefit am I trying to keep or consequence am I trying to avoid?

4) Are there ways I could get the same benefits I have now (or avoid the consequences I want to prevent) while making another choice?

5) What could I gain by choosing something else?

6) What is my decision for now?

Here's an example to help you get started:

I dislike planning all the lessons for my entire team and having them just copy off of me, but I feel like it's not a choice, because if I don't do it, none of us will have good lesson plans.

I could tell my team directly that I'm not planning by myself anymore; I could talk to my admin about it; I could ask my team leader to hold everyone accountable; I could set up co-planning sessions so we each do part of the process; I could ask them for money to purchase group licensing for curriculum resources online; I could let them not have any lesson plans and deal with the fallout.

I continue to do it all myself because I don't want to have an uncomfortable conversation, and I'm afraid the discussion wouldn't be effective. My fear is that they wouldn't write good lessons consistently and I'd end up still writing them on my own. It feels easier to do it all myself.

I probably couldn't avoid the uncomfortable conversation but I could still get high quality lessons if we co-planned. If they can do even 25% of the planning, that would reduce my workload by a quarter and save me hours every week.

If I choose to say I'm not doing this alone anymore and insist my coworkers pull their fair share, I would feel less resentful about doing all the work. I think at least one person would step up and help, thereby reducing my workload.

My decision is to talk with my coworkers about this. I'll tell them I'll finish planning the current unit, but that they need to co-plan with me for the next one. It will take a bigger investment of time up front to create a co-planning process together, but it will pay off throughout the rest of the year.

And another example:

I dislike coordinating the snacks for the soccer team but it doesn't feel like a choice because I've done it for three years and no one else wants to do it.

I could just quit and let someone else figure it out; I could tell the other parents if they want snacks for their kids they can send in their own; I could ask my spouse to share the responsibility; I could ask another parent I'm friendly with; I could set up a rotation schedule and offer to take turns with other parents; I could say I'm not doing it next season and take a break.

I haven't chosen one of these options because I don't want to upset people or risk having the kids go without snacks.

If I'm not the person doing it, that doesn't mean the kids wouldn't have snacks. And even if they didn't, it wouldn't be the end of the world. It's possible I'm the only one doing this because I'm the only one who really cares about it, and the parents would be fine with picking their kids up after practice and taking them home to eat dinner. They might not be upset with me and ultimately it doesn't matter because I don't owe them this. It is not my responsibility to make sure every child on the team has something to eat after the game.

If I say no, it would free up time and money for me each week, and also keep me from feeling resentful that I can't ever take a week off because the team is depending on me.

I'm going to approach some other parents on the team who I know are helpful, and get their opinion. Either we'll stop offering snacks or I'll ask them to take turns with me.

The power of "I choose to" instead of "I have to"

When you recognize that the way you handle your responsibilities is actually a CHOICE, you are no longer going through life mindlessly doing whatever you've always done and adding more commitments. You'll feel empowered to choose the things you want to do, engage in them in a balanced way, and figure out alternatives for everything else.

This was a big wake up call for a high school science teacher named Anna. She told me she used to complain constantly about having to spend three hours driving to and from school on a daily basis:

❝ *I finally realized if I don't want that long commute to work every day, I don't have to do it. I could quit, or I could move. If I choose not to do those things because the consequences would be worse than commuting, then I have to own my choice. Obviously there's a lot of circumstances that led me to this point, but ultimately, I choose to live and work where I do. I don't want to start over in another state where it's easier to find teaching jobs, but be far away from my extended family. I am choosing to stay here. So I have to accept that as my choice, and try to move to a higher state of being beyond complaining about how I HAVE to drive 90 minutes to work every day. I don't have to, I choose to. And feeling like it's a choice somehow makes it a little* ❞ *more bearable.*

When you perceive the way you spend your time as a choice, the limitations begin to fall away. You don't have to write off hours of time because you believe you "have" to spend them doing certain tasks. You're able to see that you're choosing to use time in that way.

So instead of defaulting to "I have to", try saying:

- I'm choosing to…
- I'm deciding to…
- I've opted to…
- I get to…

These phrases are a small shift but will help you reframe your responsibilities more accurately.

What would happen if you DIDN'T do it?

Sometimes it's hard to brainstorm alternative choices, and creating a hypothetical situation can help you get more creative.

Ask yourself, *If I had a family emergency right now or suddenly came down with the flu, would I still be forcing myself to do everything on my list today? What would I cut? What would happen if I cut it?*

This forces you to think of other possibilities. It might feel like you *have* to get groceries today, but if you were too sick to walk around the store, would you still go? Would you be able to find something to eat tonight anyway? So why not give yourself permission now — before you are so worn down that you're physically ill — to cut something out of your day?

You don't necessarily need to push the task back to another day. Just skip it altogether. If you normally get groceries on Wednesday and Saturday, skip Wednesday, scrape together meals from your pantry for a couple nights, and buy more groceries on Saturday.

Life will go on.

Anytime there's something in your workload that doesn't seem like a choice, consider what would happen if you didn't do it. Usually the consequences are not very dire, but we don't realize that until we think things through. Just explore the possible outcomes, and decide which ones you're willing to experiment with to find a better way.

Let's say that preparing materials and lessons for the week takes up your entire Sunday afternoon, and you feel like you have no choice in the matter.

And yet, your district doesn't mandate working on Sundays. Their requirement is that you have effective, thorough lesson plans. How you meet that requirement is up to you, and there are a lot of different approaches.

What would happen if you DIDN'T spend six hours every Sunday planning lessons, and decided you were going to stop after three hours, no matter what?

You might find that the tight deadline causes you to work with more focus, and you're able to get it done in half the time because you're not allowing distractions or procrastination.

Or, you might find that your materials aren't quite as good as they could have been, but ultimately, the lessons went pretty well and kids mastered the content anyway.

Worst case — your materials might not be very thorough or totally complete. What would happen then? Could you ask a coworker to share his or her plans? Could you use the same plans from last year? Could you take 10 minutes to sketch out a rough plan, then just wing it from there, using the same type of activities you used the week before?

None of these outcomes are going to ruin your life or your students' lives. They're not ideal, but then again, neither is spending six hours every Sunday prepping lesson materials.

So, it's your choice — how much time are you willing to dedicate to lesson planning? Which consequence are you choosing to deal with?

Once you make your decision, you can then figure out ways to mitigate the consequences.

Maybe you could commit to the three hour time block each Sunday for a month with a goal of figuring out more efficient ways to plan, thereby ensuring three hours *will* be sufficient for really awesome plans soon.

Or, maybe you could invest a few hours during the week to figuring out how to share the workload with another teacher, so that eventually you're only doing part of the planning work.

Or maybe you could stay late one day at school and organize your materials so it's easier to find and repurpose similar activities, instead of reinventing the wheel during your planning.

I hope you see where I'm going with this. Instead of assuming the ONLY way you can have high quality materials is to spend six hours on Sunday developing them, you can make a different choice and experiment until you find a system that works for you and your students.

Or, you can continue to give up your entire afternoon every single Sunday.

It's your choice.

And whatever you choose, if you want to be happy, you have to embrace that choice.

Maybe you really *would* rather spend six hours lesson planning, because it means you're going to be super confident in your materials and teaching will be easier throughout the week.

That's absolutely fine! You can choose to pour a lot of time into lesson planning, and compensate by looking for other aspects of your work to simplify.

But don't tell a friend, "Oh, I *can't* do anything fun on Sundays because *I have to* lesson plan." Instead say, "Sunday is the day I like to get my lesson planning done, so maybe we can hang out another time." The language you use in your self-talk and conversations has a significant impact on how you feel.

Anytime you are feeling resentful about something you've told yourself you "have to" do and can't find a way to improve things, start the process of questioning: *What would happen if I didn't do this?*

It can be a tremendously freeing exercise because it allows you to envision creative solutions that didn't seem possible when you assumed you had no choice.

Be quietly subversive when you feel like your hands are tied

One final word here about choice, because you might be thinking about the consequences you'd face with school administration if you stop doing certain things or approached your work in a different way.

The truth is that you do not have to mindlessly comply with everything you're told. You don't have to complete the 15-page lesson plan template that's technically required, or give district-mandated test prep activities every day, or follow the principal's directive to give parents your cell phone number.

You could organize with other teachers or your union to change those requirements, or approach your principal with alternative solutions, or do things your own way and hope to slide under the radar. (We'll talk more about these kinds of choices later on.)

The consequence for making a different choice could be severe and unpleasant. You might weigh the possible outcomes and decide the best choice is for you to comply.

But compliance is, in fact, a choice, as I'm sure you've noticed when giving instructions to students. Whether consciously or not, kids are always making choices about when to do what they're told, when to try to change the rules, and when to buck the system and do what they want.

Though it can be more subtle with adults, our compliance with rules and expectations is also our choice. No one can force you to spend your time and energy the way that you are.

Being in this profession was something you chose, on some level. And, you chose to accept the teaching position you were offered or assigned. You can make another choice now.

This is your job, not your whole life. You can go elsewhere, or choose not to mindlessly comply with all the requirements, or a whole host of other options. You are never completely powerless over how you spend your time.

And you should never make important decisions based on fear. A fear-based mindset will convince you that you can't question or deviate from The Plan. It leads you to feel like you can't bring your whole, true, authentic self into the building … and teaching and learning become a robotic, passionless experience for everyone in the classroom.

There is often great risk in sticking your neck out and being the one to do something different. I know this. And I'm encouraging you to do it, anyway.

Because *this is your career.*

When you were hired, someone saw potential in you to be great. You have extensive training in this field, and you got the job because you brought skills and expertise to the workplace. Your professional judgment is an asset, not a liability.

These things are all true, no matter how unvalued and untrusted you might be made to feel at times.

More importantly, *this is your life*. Viewing yourself as a victim of bureaucracy is disempowering. No one should waste their life with that mindset. You have tremendous power and value as a teacher which you must hold onto, no matter who challenges you or how.

You do not have to give away all your power. You're a professional and you have the right to assert some control over how you teach and how you use your time.

You also don't have to "do as you're told" when you're told to do something wrong. Throughout history, many lives have been lost due to those in lower areas of authority saying they were "just following orders."

Many of our teachers' and students' lives are being destroyed by the same line of reasoning. We do not have to stand by and watch the love of teaching and learning be crushed.

When you are told to do something that is clearly a waste of your time and does not benefit students in any way, resist the urge to complain or fall into a passive "I don't have a choice" state. Ask yourself, *What would happen if I didn't do it?* and consider other options.

I assure you that the best teachers I know are quietly subverting the system in this way. You'd never know they're doing it, and that's the point.

They're not trying to make a bold statement and fight back on every little thing; they're just trying to do what's best for kids. They go through the motions (or appear to be doing so), but don't let pointless policies interfere with what they or their kids need.

You have to trust your own judgment even when people in positions of authority don't empower you to do so. Hold tight to every opportunity you have to express your creativity in the classroom. Place your emotional, mental, and physical health as a top priority even when every message you hear from above is discounting your needs. Grab every single chance you get to close your door and do what's best for you and your kids.

And when the school culture makes this nearly impossible, do whatever it takes to survive while actively seeking out another position. This is your *life*. You don't have to choose to spend it in a place where you feel constantly demeaned. You are worthy of better, and change is possible for you right now.

Part Two

- ☑ I SET MY OWN EXPECTATIONS IN LIFE AND IN TEACHING
- ☐
- ☐
- ☐
- ☐

EFFECTIVENESS IS NOT ABOUT WORKING LONG HOURS. IT'S ABOUT FOCUSING ON WHAT MAKES THE BIGGEST IMPACT FOR KIDS.

I taught Vacation Bible School at our neighborhood church every summer from the time I turned sixteen until I graduated from college. VBS — which lasted just one week, and was only from 9 a.m. to 12 p.m. — wasn't a very big deal in the grand scheme of things.

But for me — a teenager who'd dreamt of being a teacher since I was little — it was a dream come true. VBS allowed me to be completely in charge of a classroom for an entire glorious week! I had (almost) total control over the learning environment and the lessons. It was the ultimate chance to play school.

This particular church had an overhead projector and a large supply of bulletin board paper, and VBS teachers would spend hours creating decorations with them. We'd first use the projector to display gigantic life-size shapes for our theme, tracing the shapes onto bulletin board paper which was taped to the wall. We'd then cut out the shapes, and finally, we'd paint them (yes, seriously) before hanging the shapes around our classrooms to immerse kids in the theme.

I loved the room transformations and enjoyed every single minute of prep work. Because this was the only VBS I'd ever taught, I assumed this was just how things were done.

It didn't occur to me until years later that we were spending 20-25 hours decorating for a program that totaled 15 hours of face time with kids.

It turned out that decorating this way isn't typical of every (or even most) VBS programs. The traceable shapes were always included with our curriculum, probably with the intent that a few would be used to decorate the entrance to the building or another common space. But I've never heard of another VBS program in which nearly every individual teacher created a total room transformation to match the different themes.

Most likely, someone many years ago had a major creative streak (plus a LOT of free time), and others loved the way the room looked so they followed suit.

At that point, it became a *tradition*. It was something that many of the teachers — myself included — looked forward to.

I don't think this practice was ever questioned during the years that I taught there, and it was certainly never questioned by me. I did it, every single year, because *that's just what teachers in our program did*. And the teachers who couldn't or didn't want to do it, well, they were sort of the odd ones out.

One of the problems with teaching in the same place for many years and not getting a chance to see other schools in action is that you can't tell what the *norm is at your school,* and what is *actually normal.*

You're never really sure what is a *requirement,* and what's *just the way it's always been done.*

When we don't have this larger perspective, we find ourselves emulating patterns that waste our time, and in a worst case scenario, aren't what's best for kids.

> *Since everyone's doing things the same way, we don't think to question THEM, and instead begin to question ourselves: "All my colleagues are fine with this. Am I making a big deal out of nothing? Am I wrong to think we should be doing things a different way?"*

To question school norms and do your own thing — particularly when you are depending on the job for your livelihood — requires a lot of confidence in your teaching methodology. It also takes the courage to believe that you can be who you decide to be, rather than letting others' expectations define you.

In this section of the book, we'll dig into the mindset which gives rise to that courage. We'll discuss how to develop a deep confidence in your instructional approach through continual self-reflection. We'll also look at how to develop the courage to challenge expectations in your personal life, relationships, family, and home.

But, let's begin with examining norms in the workplace so you can differentiate between what's truly necessary and what's always been done.

4

Questioning norms in school culture

I've had the privilege of being a full-time classroom teacher in eight different schools and working as a part-time instructional coach in dozens more.

Let's just say I have *seen some things*.

Every single site — even ones within the same community with similar student demographics — had very, very different school cultures. Each of the following things was considered normal in at least one school I've worked in:

- Having students call teachers by their first names to show equality
- Having students stand up when an adult entered the room to show respect for authority

- Not issuing consequences to students after they've physically assaulted the teacher
- Suspending students for rolling their eyes at the teacher
- Keeping classroom doors locked at all times
- Keeping classroom doors propped open at all times
- Inviting parents to observe whenever they want
- Not allowing parents to enter the classroom for any reason during the school day

In many cases, norms are not objectively right or wrong. They're just standard expectations which are baked into the school culture.

Some norms have developed organically over time, and others have been forced into place through a clear and intentional agenda. Some norms happen as a direct result of administrative leadership, and some happen despite the principal wanting things to be different.

There are many factors which create a school culture, but the main point for our purposes here is this: *What's normal at your school is not normal universally.*

It's specific to your country, region, district, community, school leaders, faculty, parents, and students. The people, place, and time all impact the norms at your school.

And this means that norms are malleable, not immutable. Norms are not destined to stay the same forever.

Even more importantly, it means a single person has the power to *disrupt* norms.

A pair or small group of people have the power to begin *shifting* norms.

So, the expectations in your school do not have to define who you are as a teacher or how you spend your time. You can choose to define these things for yourself.

Who said it has to be done that way?

I have no problem going along with school norms if they fit my personality and don't have a negative impact on students. But if the expectation doesn't make sense to me, I can't help but question it.

Folks with my personality type need a logical and practical reason for doing what we've been told. If we don't want to do something, we're going to ask why it needs to be done. We won't comply with norms we dislike unless we're absolutely sure there is no alternative, and even then, we're likely to find ways to insert our own approach whenever possible.

If being a questioner is not your natural tendency, you can train yourself to think in this way when you're faced with expectations that aren't useful to you or your students. It can be as simple as considering these 4 questions:

1. *What, specifically, do I believe is required of me?*
2. *Who is requiring this?*
3. *Why are they requiring this?*
4. *How can I meet the requirement in a way that works better for me and my students?*

I'll share an example based on a coaching call I did with a special education teacher, who said she was spending about 10 hours a week correcting errors on student papers.

I began by asking her specifically what is required. She answered that she needs to add every missing punctuation mark, capitalize all the incorrect lowercase letters, fix every grammatical mistake, etc. for all of her students' work. Understandably, she was frustrated with the immense amount of time this was taking.

Having gotten clear on the perceived requirement, I moved on to the next question. "Who said you have to proofread and edit every single paper your students touch?"

She paused. "I don't know, actually. I never really thought about it."

"So is there a chance you're spending 10 hours a week on something you don't actually have to do?"

"Hmm. I mean ... maybe ... "

We needed to get to the bottom of where this perceived requirement had originated, since it wasn't a clear directive. "Who told you this was a requirement?"

"Nobody, really. The other special ed teacher said this is the way she does it and she showed me how."

"And who told her to do it that way?"

"I ... don't really know. I think she said that's how the teacher who had my position before did it."

"So there's no one in the school or district who's mandating this?"

She thought carefully about it. "No, I guess not."

Together, we uncovered the truth: this "requirement" was just a tradition, most likely put in place by a teacher who wanted to ensure students were aware of their errors (or didn't want parents to feel mistakes had been overlooked).

I wanted to see if there was a better way to achieve that outcome. "What would happen if you didn't correct all the errors?"

"I think ... probably nothing. The kids don't even look at the corrections. They just stuff the papers in their backpacks and take them home."

"What do you *want* the kids to do?"

"Well, I'd like them to look over the corrections I made and learn from them, and use them to improve their writing."

"And the way you're doing things now — that's not the result you're getting. It's not impacting their learning in a positive way, AND it's taking up way too much time, AND you're not required to do it."

"Yes."

"So this means … you don't really have to."

"Yeah. Wow. So I guess we can figure out a way that puts more responsibility on the kids, instead of having me just fix everything for them."

I have a variation on this conversation almost every single week in the 40 Hour Teacher Workweek Club. I believe *every* teacher is doing things s/he believes are required but could be streamlined, simplified or eliminated.

No one is exempt. I once spent *two entire school years* documenting intervention strategies in a useless and time-intensive way.

Why? Because I didn't realize the directive no longer applied once we got a new superintendent. I was complaining about it to my team one day and discovered I was the only one still detailing the strategies, instead of using new codes which had abbreviations and could be written in a fraction of the time.

We all have to practice questioning the status quo, and train ourselves to turn complaints into questions.

What, specifically, do I believe is required of me? Who is requiring this? Why are they requiring this? How can I meet the requirement in a way that works better for me and my students?

Find more efficient and effective ways to meet the requirements

The people creating mandates in your district have probably never received training in productivity strategies or time management. They are simply working within the norms of school bureaucracy, which tends to be full of unnecessary paperwork for "risk management" purposes.

Additionally, the decision-makers are extremely busy. Like you, if they find something that seems somewhat workable, they'll usually go with that and move on to putting out the next fire. They don't always have the time or capacity to figure out optimal solutions which minimize unnecessary work for teachers, nor is that their highest priority.

This can actually be good news for you, because it means your higher-ups aren't married to the process. They have a desired outcome in mind, and the current procedure is just one way to accomplish that outcome.

If you can uncover the *real* goal behind the requirement and find a more efficient, effective way to get that outcome, you may be able to create change.

In other words, don't assume somebody higher up thought that whatever's driving you nuts was the best or ultimate plan. It might have just been a band-aid solution to whatever bigger issue they needed to address, and so they rolled it out. And that means if you have a better solution to present, it will make their job easier, because they can meet their objectives *and* keep teachers happy. It's a win-win.

Let's say you can only give kids 10 minutes of recess. Ask yourself why. It's probably not because school leadership believes recess is bad, but because they want to make sure kids are getting every possible moment of instructional time, and this seemed like an easy way to ensure that (or make it look like that on paper for stakeholders who are pressuring them).

If you can find a way to achieve that outcome of maximizing instructional time AND incorporate movement outdoors, there might be some leeway.

I did this with my second graders one year in a district that banned recess past first grade. (I *know*.) Even though the school was under tremendous pressure to raise its "D" score, I was able to find ways to get my kids outside for 15 minutes every day with my principal's blessing.

I understood that the real goal of the no-recess requirement was to avoid wasting instructional time so we could improve test scores. So, I didn't focus too much on proving the benefits of recess to my principal. I just focused on the outcome I knew she was under tremendous pressure to achieve.

I said I wanted to conduct some action research to test my theory that students would concentrate (and thereby perform) better after a movement break. I asked her to let me try taking the kids out for fresh air and exercise daily for three weeks. If our weekly benchmark tests showed any drop or my students weren't progressing at the rate of the other second grade classes, recess would be discontinued.

In an outcome that will surprise no teacher ever, recess turned out to be highly beneficial for my students. Because their benchmark scores maintained or improved overall, recess became a regular part of our day. Soon, some of the other second grade teachers began doing the same thing.

And to my knowledge, no one from the district ever noticed or questioned this, probably because the school was improving its scores and that was the measure they were using for effectiveness. No one was measuring how much time we were spending outdoors and there was no reason for them to ask, as long as we were meeting our academic goals.

Brainstorm alternatives to school norms

Let's take another example. Maybe the norm in your school is to hold faculty meetings every Thursday after dismissal, and you usually find them to be a waste of time.

Ask yourself — why are meetings held every Thursday? It's probably not because the principal is convinced this is the most effective way to disseminate important information.

It's just the way we've always "done meetings" and no one ever figured out a better approach. If you can find an alternative way to achieve that outcome of keeping people informed, you might be able to reduce the number of meetings.

It's simply a matter of solving the problem in a different way:

The norm in our school is A, for the purpose of B.
Alternative ways to achieve B could be C, D, E, or F.

Brainstorm these alternatives together when you can — either as a staff, team, or just with one other teacher you trust. You could even brainstorm with teachers in a private group online or with friends who teach in other schools. Sometimes outside perspectives can be even more useful because those educators don't feel constrained by the norms in your school.

No idea is too unfeasible or stupid to write down, because an outlandish possibility that one person imagines could spur a suggestion later that's more workable. Write down everything you can think of, in this case, to reduce the burden of those Thursday meetings after school:

- Send a summary email instead of the meeting when there's no teacher input required
- Meet during your lunch break or planning period instead of after school
- Alternate 10-minute meetings and hour-long meetings so that every other week, you're disseminating super urgent

announcements and the more detailed work is tackled in two meetings a month

- Have someone record a screencast of important info for teachers to watch when it's convenient for them rather than meeting in person
- Send important info via email before the meeting so you don't have to review as much information in person
- Change the expectation so you only meet when there is something to meet about (rather than just automatically showing up every week)
- Use a polling tool online instead of showing up in person to vote on issues
- Share ideas in a Google Doc and collaborate virtually before the meeting so all you have to do in person is make final decisions
- Identify which staff members don't need to attend each meeting and make it optional for them
- Structure meetings so the info that applies to everyone is shared first, and folks who don't need to stay can leave

Write down all the ideas, and then discuss them. Which ones could you try out or present to your administrators as an alternative?

Enter this undertaking with a spirit of determination. Do not give up if there are no easy solutions or if you encounter resistance even among your fellow teachers. It's okay if there is no permanent solution to eliminating all meetings. If you can reduce the length or frequency of even a couple meetings, that will save you hours of time.

The real value here is in the brainstorming and experimentation. You're practicing the shift from complaining to questioning. You're no longer just sitting back and allowing other people to waste your time. You are being proactive.

You're using your professional judgement, leadership skills, and expertise to find better solutions that improve working conditions for the entire faculty. You are refusing to passively allow a bureaucracy to steal your enthusiasm for your work.

Questioning and considering alternative solutions is always going to be more empowering than assuming you have no choice in how things are done.

3 ways to respond to school norms you dislike

Once you've done some brainstorming, there are three basic approaches you can use to tackle the problem in a new way. You might move forward on your own or organize with other teachers. I'll give a personal example of each.

1. Get over it, and do it with a good attitude.

I had transferred to a new school one year, and discovered that teachers there were required to let students in their rooms 20 minutes before the first bell. This cut into our prep time every single day. Not being a morning person, this was a big deal for me, as I needed that time to gear up. I talked to my colleagues, and they said teachers had questioned this in the past and the principal had been adamant. My team leader indicated that the best solution was to go along with it, and train kids to come in the room and work quietly so that we could continue to work, too.

So I did. I didn't love the situation, but I decided not to complain about it. I accepted it as part of the job and moved on. I did not think to myself every day, *"This is so unfair. I can't believe she's taking up my prep time every morning like this."* I didn't look for little ways to remind the principal of how much I was sacrificing whenever I was asked to do something else.

Instead, I reframed it as something I was choosing to tolerate and therefore wasn't going to waste more time thinking about. Every job requires extra responsibilities you don't feel like doing. Choosing to accept something you don't like is a viable path to relieving the stress around that task because you're no longer expending energy on resisting it.

2. Quietly subvert the system.

This same principal also asked us to participate in a rotation for afternoon bus duty. In South Florida, this meant I'd have to stand in the sun and humidity during the hottest part of the day for 30 minutes, dripping with sweat, and again lose out on my planning time. I did it for a month and couldn't take it anymore. At least with morning duty, I was able to work in my air conditioned classroom.

I discussed things with my team, and it was clear that teachers would have to help out. The principal didn't have any other options, unless we somehow found funding for a bunch of aides in the afternoon. Advocating for that seemed like a difficult path, so I asked my colleagues if someone would be willing to do my bus duty for me, in exchange for me taking over a responsibility of their choice.

To my surprise, one of them replied, "I don't understand why you hate bus duty. It's a nice break, hanging out with the kids and talking to parents. I'll do it for you, if you run my photocopies for me."

Um, yes, please! That was an easy trade.

I was already in the office every morning anyway, and running 60 copies instead of 30 was no skin off my back. To my colleague — who hated dealing with the malfunctioning copier and found herself trapped in endless conversations with folks in the office — this was a terrific deal.

And so I never had to do bus duty again. I can't remember if we even told our principal about this arrangement, but I know we didn't ask permission. Bus duty was not something admin assigned because she wanted each of us to suffer equally. I doubt she really cared who was out there, as long as there was coverage daily and teachers came to an agreement without creating problems for her. My colleague and I worked together to quietly subvert the system and use our time in a way that made sense for us.

3. Speak up.

Later that year in the spring, I left the building after dismissal and discovered my car was not where I thought I'd left it. I wandered around the lot, confused about where I might have parked. I reached into my bag to get my keys so I could set off the alarm and determine the car's location … and realized the keys were not in my bag. Oh, and neither was my wallet! I slowly realized that at some point during the school day, someone had come into my classroom, stolen my wallet and keys, and driven off in my car.

Eventually, we realized the theft had happened during dismissal. I learned that all the entrances to the building were left unlocked and *we had no cameras anywhere other than the front gate.* I had assumed cameras were a standard thing and was horrified at how incredibly unsafe this situation was.

The principal repeatedly insisted the district did not have funds for cameras, and we'd have to make sure our personal belongings were better secured and our classroom doors locked at all times.

However, I felt obligated to press on the issue of better security.

I calmly and professionally insisted to the principal, in a staff meeting, and in a PTA meeting that we could not accept "no" from the district when it came to funding for this. Many of our hallways in Florida were not enclosed, and we desperately needed cameras to record activity since we'd had multiple break-ins, and thousands of dollars of technology had been stolen just a few weeks prior to that. I wanted this latest violation to be a wake-up call that crimes were now being committed while students were still on campus, and that risk was unacceptable.

Note that I did not turn this into my life's work, aim to become a community hero, or lose sleep every night feeling outraged until my mission was fulfilled. I simply helped get the gears grinding toward change by speaking up in a couple of meetings. It took another year for the paperwork and funding to be processed, but more security measures were eventually put in place, and I was satisfied that I had done my part in getting people in charge to take the situation more seriously.

Avoid being labeled "the angry teacher" by showing up with solutions

I hope these examples illustrate that you can exercise your agency without doing so in an angry, bitter, loud, or demanding way. Certainly you can speak from a place of righteous rage if that feels warranted and productive, but it's not a necessity.

When we talk about questioning norms and self-advocacy, that doesn't mean marching into the principal's office and saying, "How dare you ask me to tutor students for free during my lunch break? I'm absolutely not doing that no matter what you say, and I'll go to the union if you try to make me."

You don't have to be defensive and reactive. You are not a helpless child whose only recourse is to throw a tantrum and hope the parent gives in.

You're a talented professional who was selected to do this job. You have legitimate wants, needs, ideas, and solutions, and you deserve to be taken seriously.

Go vent to a friend, and get all that negative emotion out before you walk into your principal's office. Then you can show up feeling confident in who you are and what you bring to the table:

> *I'd like to talk about the request for faculty to tutor during our lunch breaks. Can I let you know my thoughts on that — is this a good time? As you know, I'm an introvert. My lunch breaks are my time to recharge and decompress. When I don't have 20 minutes to myself during the day, I feel like students don't get my best in the afternoon. I'm concerned that if I tutor during lunch, the quality of my lesson delivery will suffer, because it's not possible to provide outstanding instruction for six hours straight each day. I realize you're in a crunch here. Is there some other way I can help out without compromising my break? I have a couple ideas that might work, if you'd like to hear them.*

The purpose of approaching your administration in this way is not to let them know how unfair they're being and how overworked you are. The purpose is to create change, and you don't need pity or even empathy from your school leaders in order to do that.

So, try to choose a professional approach that is focused on getting the results you want, not on "being heard." Don't hope that dumping your emotions on your principal will persuade (or guilt trip) him or her into figuring out an alternative. Take charge and tell your principal the solution you want!

It's a bit like the relationship advice we hear about not expecting spouses or partners to read our minds. If you want something from your partner, ask for it directly. Don't just tell them what they're not doing and how unhappy you are. What, specifically, do you need and what would that look like?

You can communicate without blame, judgment, or heated emotions. When the other person understands exactly what your needs are and how they could be met, you're on the path to figuring out a solution together.

Of course, this is easier said than done. Many of us are not comfortable with speaking up for ourselves in this way at work because we're not used to doing it in any arena of life. We hold in our resentment, or lash out in emotionally manipulative ways, such as by being passive-aggressive.

This feels safer to us. The expectation for women in particular is that our communication style should be sweet and polite, rather than direct. The feelings of the listener should be prioritized over our own.

Most people are used to women conforming to this social pressure to prioritize niceness over authenticity. So, when we do get the courage to be forthright about what we need, we know we run the risk of being perceived as rude, demanding, aggressive, defensive, overly emotional, fragile, irrational, or unstable. Our concerns may be dismissed and we may get a condescending response that invalidates our experience and feelings.

Many of us have witnessed this firsthand. We know teachers who have stood up for themselves and were perceived as difficult. They got labeled as "not a team player" or "not a good fit for the school" and have been blackballed because of it.

However, when you prepare an approach that is professional, level-headed, and solution-oriented, you can counteract these issues. It's not a fool-proof method, but it does inoculate you quite a bit from the negative labels.

In fact, if you handle the situation in a professional, solution-oriented way, your "complaint" can actually turn you into one of the most valuable members of the faculty. Most of your colleagues will just talk about the problem behind the principal's back. You, on the other hand, are approaching the principal directly with actual solutions.

The principal probably knows teachers are unhappy. Others have expressed that in a myriad of subtle and not-so-subtle ways. But you might be the only one with the courage and professionalism to offer up your expertise to your principal, and join as a partner in figuring out solutions.

This is possible even if your principal does not have the reputation of being an approachable leader. That's because being an admin of any kind is a bit lonely — they don't have anyone else in the building at their level of the hierarchy. They can't say how they really feel because everyone reports to them, and they need to behave as the leader. Administrators often feel like they alone bear the burden of making hard decisions and dealing with the fallout.

You can choose to show up as an ally to your administrator(s) and be a sounding board when tough decisions need to be made. Approach them with several possible solutions, and focus the conversation on what can be done rather than detailing the problem. Over time, your principal will be more likely to develop trust in you and take your input seriously.

Even if your ideas are not accepted, you will leave the room with more insight as to the obstacles your principal is facing. Often regulations that seem unreasonable to teachers have some solid rationale or extenuating circumstances behind them, and once you can see the big picture that your principal does, you'll understand how things defaulted to the way they are, and just how challenging it is to make everyone happy.

A caveat to consider, though: Approaching your principal as a solution-oriented problem solver has to be done in a very genuine way and with confidence in your ideas. It will backfire if you are manipulative or passive-aggressive, and will come across as insincere if you make threats.

You must genuinely want to work with your administrators to find a mutually acceptable solution, and enter the discussion with an authentic respect for their perspective. If you can't end the conversation with a solution, the goal is to leave with an open door to bring back more solutions later and continue talking until things are resolved.

How privilege and reputation can be used to disrupt the status quo

I will acknowledge that privilege plays a role in being able to question norms. As a teacher, I was young, friendly-looking, warm, personable, and of course, a white woman, so I was not under any special scrutiny by default.

I looked the part, and I fit in easily. That made it easier for me to fly under the radar because the general impression was that I was the typical nice, "normal" teacher.

That's a privilege based almost entirely on my appearance and people's assumptions about me, and it's a privilege not everyone has. It's part of the reason why I felt it was worth pursuing change — I had a responsibility to speak up. I could do so, and not all of my colleagues felt the same, for a wide variety of reasons.

There are a lot of biases and prejudices that can impact who "gets away with things" in a school and who's put under a microscope.

Sometimes it's just a matter of who the administrators are related to or friends with, or who they like and who they don't.

So if you're one of the gang, resist the tendency to blend in or avoid making waves. Being part of the dominant or majority group is a privilege, and you can use that privilege to advocate for better working conditions for everyone.

Another thing that made it easier for me to speak up was my reputation in the building. I doubt I was perceived as a go-with-the-flow kind of teacher, and was never the principal's pet.

But that usually didn't matter, because I had the reputation of being *good at my job.*

I don't think I did anything exceptional. I was just creative and competent and caring. My lessons were dependably solid and my classroom management was strong. My administrators never had to worry that I wasn't teaching or that I'd say something inappropriate to families or students.

I was achieving the outcome that everyone wanted from me — getting the majority of kids to make 10 months' growth in 10 months' time. Compared to everything else my admin had to deal with, I was the least of their concerns.

So, sometimes — even though this is not always enough — one of the best ways to stand in your power and not let others' expectations define you is to focus on being an outstanding teacher. Regardless of who you are, what biases are working against you, or how you are currently perceived, I believe this is the most important thing to focus on when you want more leeway to question school norms.

Make your classroom a place that is welcoming, clean, and organized. Develop a good rapport with students and make sure they're making solid learning progress. Build relationships with parents so you're not getting serious complaints. Have a good attitude in the hallway and at staff meetings (smile, greet people, encourage people, share resources).

In other words, show up each day with enthusiasm for your work.

 YOU'LL HAVE SO MUCH MORE CREDIBILITY WHEN YOU QUESTION THE STATUS QUO IF EVERYTHING IN YOUR DEMEANOR AND TEACHING PRACTICE DECLARES WORDLESSLY, "I AM HERE TO DO A GREAT JOB FOR KIDS."

Pour your energy into things that really move the needle for your students. Don't complain about every little thing or resist every single change. Do some of the stuff you don't want to do, and be supportive and positive around your coworkers.

And then, when something truly crosses the line for you, speak up in a reasonable, assertive way.

Lead colleagues toward change and support those who speak up

Most of the examples I've given so far have been norms established and perpetuated by those in charge. In these cases, teachers can work together to find better solutions.

But what happens when a damaging norm is upheld by your coworkers?

There were a number of instances when I had to go against my colleagues. One of the most important times occurred during my second year of teaching, when I transferred from an elementary school to an early childhood center in our district where I'd be teaching HeadStart (three- and four-year-olds).

I loved my new school, but in mid-September, I discovered that all the classes re-enacted their teachers' interpretation of the first

Thanksgiving, and had students dress up as "Indians" to do mock pow-wows.

This stereotypical and historically inaccurate teaching disturbed me greatly, but I wasn't sure what to do about it. I asked a couple of colleagues if the celebration bothered any of them, and was repeatedly met with blank stares.

I persisted until I found a colleague who also found it problematic, and though she didn't want to take the lead on speaking up, she encouraged me to call the district's Diversity and Multicultural Department.

I had no idea such a department existed, so I was thrilled when the woman in charge helped us figure out what to say to our team members. She even offered to come to our school to support us in the conversation.

The next time we had a team meeting, my voice was shaking, but I told my colleagues I felt uncomfortable with the school tradition. I admitted I wasn't sure about the more appropriate way to teach preschoolers about Thanksgiving, so I'd asked the district to provide us with some resources, and introduced the woman who I'd invited to our meeting (with my team leader's permission).

I think we all got a tremendous education that day. Many of my colleagues probably thought I was presumptuous or ridiculous, and didn't see the big deal. Some of them probably disliked me from then on.

But I knew in my heart that their good intentions did not prevent a harmful impact. Our school tradition involved miseducating children and perpetuating inaccurate stereotypes, and I needed to offer my colleagues support in doing better.

The entire way we taught Thanksgiving changed that year. There were no more "I is for Indian" posters in the alphabet displays on the wall, no more native "costumes" made of paper bags, and no more war chief mimicry.

Because this school was for kids age 0-5 with developmental delays, a more in-depth and authentic exploration of the topic would have been quite difficult, so we focused on being grateful and enjoying a Thanksgiving meal together at lunch. The kids sang songs about being thankful, and dressed up as turkeys instead of "Indians."

As I continue to learn more about other people's identities and life choices, I can consider further work to be done. I'm more cognizant now of the number of families who are vegan, as well as the fact that not all students celebrate Thanksgiving and it's considered a day of mourning for many indigenous people.

However, this was a big move in the right direction for all of us, particularly back in 2001 when the mainstream conversations around these issues were different than they are today. It takes time to shift teachers' long-held belief systems, whether it's on an issue like this, or eliminating homework, or moving away from punitive discipline policies.

Since I was just 22, I was too naive and unversed in school politics to realize it at the time, but speaking up caused my colleagues to view me as a leader.

Whether they agreed with me was irrelevant: I'd proven that I was not afraid to stick my neck out. My colleagues knew that was a valuable quality to have in a teammate, given how many things they were unhappy with but tolerated because they didn't want to rock the boat.

There was — and still is — a desperate need for more educators to disrupt the status quo. Everyone is looking for leadership. They want someone to decide they're not going to stand by and continue to watch teachers be exploited and children be harmed.

You can be that leader, and you don't have to do it alone. Even though I spearheaded this change in my school, I didn't do it by myself. I never would have had the courage to speak up if I hadn't found that one colleague — a true leader in the school already — who encouraged me and backed me up in that meeting. And, it was the woman from our district who clearly articulated the problem and presented better solutions to our staff.

Someone just has to *initiate* the change. Someone has to be the first to question things. Someone has to say, "I'll take the lead and speak up first."

In the instances when you feel like it can't or shouldn't be you, have the courage to stand with those who are advocating on behalf of teachers and kids. Don't listen silently to a colleague's objections in a staff meeting, then thank them privately afterward because you share their concerns.

Instead, visibly nod while they're speaking, raise your hand to add an additional point, and make it clear in front of your admin and colleagues that you have their back. *Then* thank them afterward and ask what you can do to support the cause going forward. We can't let the same handful of teachers do all the heavy lifting, and make themselves vulnerable while everyone else says nothing.

Standing up for what you know is right is an important part of true leadership. You're not trying to be a complainer, hater, troublemaker, bully, or rabble-rouser. You're being a leader.

You're rallying people to overcome an injustice, fix an inequity, or make sure that the situation is no longer harmful to teachers or kids.

In true leadership, there can be no ulterior motives, self-righteousness, passive-aggressive power plays, retribution, or ganging up in cliques. Your motive must be pure, and the change initiated with compassion and sincere desire to help everyone involved.

You do not have to bribe, threaten, or force your colleagues or administrators to change. That's nearly impossible when you have no authority over them, anyway. Instead, you can lead them, by inspiring and encouraging them to be their best.

When you advocate for change in this way, you will feel good about yourself regardless of the outcome (which you can't control). You'll know you did what you believed was right, and did so in an honest and constructive way.

Resist the "school family" manipulation

I recognize that being seen as a leader in your school can be scary, because an unwanted spotlight is placed on you. When your leadership involves going against colleagues, it's even more perilous.

That's particularly true if you have been conditioned to believe that your colleagues are part of your "school family." It's going to be quite painful to do anything that creates dissent or tension amongst "family members."

Of course, I am not opposed to cultivating a family-like atmosphere in schools. The school family analogy can feel wonderful when you've just had a baby or lost a family member. It conveys the sentiment that you are loved and supported like family.

However, it's extremely difficult to carve out your own path or question traditions within a family. If you see something problematic happening in school (such as biased treatment toward a particular demographic of students, or ineffective, damaging teaching practices) speaking up means you have to be willing to break from "the family."

Additionally, this school family analogy can be used to manipulate you into mopping the hallways, giving up your lunch break to conduct unpaid cafeteria duty, or attending mandatory evening events. "We are a school family" can be code for "You are expected to spend your free time going above and beyond with no compensation."

A family dynamic increases the pressure to go along with the status quo or provide additional unpaid labor. You might not stay until 6 p.m. stapling together theater programs for someone who's just a coworker, but if your family needs you ... of course you'll do it!

Professionalism flies out the window when you're dealing with family. Professionals are compensated for their time and expertise. Family members carry out traditions without asking why. They just pitch in and do whatever needs to be done.

The school family framing plays on what Seth Nichols termed *The Women's Honor Code*. Remember that from section one? Anything for the kids, no matter the cost. You'll find yourself neglecting your health, relationships, home, and even your own kids because your "school family" needs you.

If you don't go along with the status quo, the implicit (though rarely spoken) accusation is that you are breaking the honor code:

You're letting kids down. Children will suffer because of you. Don't you care about your students? What kind of heartless monster are you? Why even go into this profession if you don't really want to help kids?

That's a family, all right ... a really dysfunctional one in which people manipulate one another through passive-aggression and thinly veiled threats.

This kind of pressure can come from your administrators, your colleagues, or both. Regardless, you do not have to participate in the dysfunction. Your primary obligation at work is to serve the students who are assigned to you by teaching them well. Give your all in that capacity.

And when your "school family" asks you to go along with ridiculous requests because it would upset your teammates otherwise, or they hand off so many responsibilities that it interferes with your ability to teach your classes?

That's when you may choose to say no.

The reality is that your school is your workplace. You can care about and support everyone in the building, and certain colleagues can feel like family to you, but your school is a *community*, not a family.

You are together in that school because you are professionals, not because you are relatives or best friends. It is not your job to maintain close friendships with your colleagues or make sure everyone likes you. You can do the work of teaching you were hired for and then go home to your real or chosen family.

So when you hear the phrase "school family," reflect on the context. Is it being used to show love and support when you need it most, or is it an attempt to keep you from questioning norms and exploit you for more free labor?

Dismantle the false "team player" obligations

Rarely have I regretted times when I worked extra hours to do things for the benefit of my students. If I spent my evenings and weekends on tasks that mattered or were fulfilling, I didn't really mind.

Bitterness and exhaustion showed up when I got roped into more committee work, extracurriculars, lunch duty, meetings, paperwork, and data entry.

 IN OTHER WORDS, I DIDN'T MIND GOING ABOVE AND BEYOND FOR MY STUDENTS. WHAT BOTHERED ME WAS BEING GUILT-TRIPPED INTO GOING ABOVE AND BEYOND FOR THE *INSTITUTION OF SCHOOL*.

My loyalty and affection were reserved for the kids, not for the school system which froze my pay steps, increased my work obligations, and crowded more students into my classroom with every passing year.

Because the government does not fully fund our educational systems, it relies on anyone and everyone who works in a school to pick up the slack together. All the extra work that's outside your standard teaching duties *should* be handled by someone who's trained and paid to do it.

Your school deserves aides to handle supervision duties during non-instructional time.

Your school deserves instructional coaches to support teachers in curriculum mapping and lesson design.

Your school deserves a testing coordinator who tracks data, and uses that data to help inform more staff who will pull out students for additional support.

Instead, these tasks (and dozens more) must be taken on by people who are already working more than a full time job as a classroom teacher. In the best case scenario, staff might be offered a stipend that averages out to $5 an hour.

And if you don't participate in this racket, you may be accused of "not being a team player."

This mentality is so insidious that we internalize it and repeat it back to one another. For example, I recently saw a teacher leave this comment on a blog post about creating boundaries:

"In most schools, teachers would be pink-slipped if they say no to committee work. It brings down the morale of the school if you don't. You have to be seen as a team player."

Taken at face value, that comment might resonate. But it's inaccurate to say that most (not just some, but *most*) principals will fire a teacher who is effective in every way simply because that person limits their committee work to only what's required.

If your principal tries to get rid of you because of this, it's probably the final straw after a long list of (real or perceived) infractions, and the root problem is much bigger. Most principals want to hold onto good teachers and are not looking for reasons to replace them.

The real threat here is the line about "bringing down the morale of the school." This is a veiled reference to *other teachers'* opinions. It points to a fear that colleagues are going to be resentful if you say no because they'll have to do the work if you don't. (We'll get to that in a moment.)

The reference to morale — coupled with the line about needing to be "seen as a team player" — implies that saying yes to every committee somehow ensures you'll be viewed as pulling your weight:

If you want to keep your job and make sure your colleagues don't hate you, then do as you're told. We're trapped with each other in these working conditions and everyone has to suffer equally together.

Of course, excessive committee work is not synonymous with being a team player. We all know teachers who serve on multiple committees yet have such a negative attitude that they bring down morale everywhere they go.

And, committees aren't the defining element — there are many other ways to pitch in and contribute to the school community.

Being a team player does not mean saying yes to everything you're asked to do. It's about knowing when to go along with a good attitude, when to quietly subvert the system, and when to demonstrate leadership skills by speaking up and confidently saying no.

Break the barrel instead of pulling each other down

Why don't teachers stand together to challenge expectations that are harmful for kids and for ourselves?

Why do we pressure each other to uphold the expectations for unpaid labor, instead of collectively pushing back against the system?

Why do we warn one another about the risks involved with setting boundaries, and actively discourage colleagues from ever daring to insist on better working conditions?

You can't do that at our school.

That would never work.

Teachers can't get away with that.

You'll get fired if you do that.

Parents will complain.

The district frowns upon that.

We perpetuate a system in which teachers are constantly fearful of advocating for themselves.

We're afraid that if a colleague is able to do a good job while working reasonable hours and we aren't, there's something wrong with us, or we made a career mistake in choosing the grade level and subject area we did. It doesn't feel *fair* when colleagues manage to simplify and we can't find a way to do it, too.

We're also afraid that if one teacher dares to create boundaries, that will leave all the rest of the staff to make up for it.

If you say no to bus duty, I have to do it.

If you say no to the committee, I'll have to join it.

If one teacher finds a way out, all the others will be stuck with the additional workload.

Like crabs in a barrel — in which anyone could feasibly escape — teachers will pull each other down so that no one can get out of a bad situation. If one has to stay and be miserable, so do all of us. The implication is:

Who are you to be happy? Who are you to have a life apart from work? Who are you to go home and enjoy time with your family? If I have to grade papers until midnight, you should, too. Stop looking for an "easy way out." We all agreed to be overworked and underappreciated when we took this job — who are you to buck the rules?

This is the mentality that keeps us from ever creating change. We don't support each other in work-life balance, because when a colleague draws the line, we aren't willing to draw the line, too. We grumble about it ("must be nice to leave at 3 o'clock") but we're not happy for our colleagues, and we aren't inspired by them to take charge of our lives, too.

I've fallen into this trap myself many times. Remember that suggestion about structuring meetings so that general info is shared first, and those who don't need the remaining info are allowed to leave early? I recall one of my principals doing that, and all of us teachers were absolutely furious about it.

I complained to my team, "It's so unfair that K-2 teachers don't have to stay for this meeting just because they don't give the test! It's bad enough that 3rd-5th grades are responsible for giving the test, and now we have extra meetings while they get to go home?"

Looking back, I am ashamed of that reaction. I would rather have had all my colleagues sit and suffer with me than be happy that at least some of us could leave on time after a long day. What a warped mentality — and I didn't even realize it because we all thought like that. It was our school norm.

The bigger picture was that I was already resentful because I was being held responsible for my third graders' test scores when so much of what my students knew was a direct result of what had happened (or not happened) in the kids' K-2 years. Because those grade levels weren't tested, all the responsibility was on *me*, and now I had more meetings too? So infuriating.

Meanwhile, because our salary bonuses were based on test scores and only teachers in grades 3-5 were testing their kids, the K-2 teachers felt powerless. Sure, they got to leave the meeting early, but their pay checks were going to be determined by the work that other teachers were doing. It didn't matter how hard *they'd* worked. If I and the other 3-5 teachers didn't "pull our weight," the K-2 teachers' pay checks would suffer.

Can you see how this system is set up to turn us against each other?

We felt powerless to change the system, so we used each other as scapegoats for our unhappiness.

We complained and gossiped about one another. We compared our workloads and competed for the prized martyr title of Most Difficult Job in the School, while looking down on anyone who had an "easier" teaching position or wasn't sacrificing for the school every moment like we were.

> We were like crabs in a barrel, pulling each other down so that none of us could escape. And tragically, we never focused our energy where it should have been: on the folks who built the barrel and trapped us inside.

A barrel is not a crab's natural habitat. The "crabs in a barrel" phenomenon only manifests when crabs are forced into an environment where they're isolated from the resources needed for survival.

As teachers, we don't need to help each other escape the barrel. We need to break down the barrel so we can be free to thrive.

Stop holding in resentment until you just burn out

Many teachers do not organize, advocate for themselves, or draw boundaries in any way for years upon years. They fight each other for limited resources and settle for scraps. They work themselves to the bone, complain endlessly in the staff room, and never actually speak up for what they need in order to create change.

And then one day, there's some small straw that breaks the camel's back, and they make the decision to quit. That's it. They're done. They can't take it anymore. They'd rather work for minimum wage somewhere than take the abuse any longer.

They never spoke up because they were afraid of jeopardizing their job, and instead, either suffered for years until life circumstances allowed them to quit, or moved heaven and earth to make it possible for them to leave.

Can you see the irony here?

The job was so valuable that they didn't want to risk it by insisting their needs be met ... but in the end, the job wasn't valuable at all, because it morphed into something that was destroying them.

What if you stop the pattern by setting some boundaries and saying no right now?

What if you don't let it get so bad that you have to leave the profession altogether?

If you're contemplating the risk of leaving, why not contemplate the risk of improving the workplace before it gets to that point?

When you stand up for what's right, you make things better for the teachers around you. You set the precedent for them. You empower them to see that change is possible so they can learn to stand up for themselves, too.

Why not contribute to the "school family" in this way before you quit? If you can remove one unreasonable request from teachers' workload, isn't that a victory? Doesn't that pave the way for other teachers to fight, too?

Don't just hold in the resentment until you burn out or walk out. You can be the person you want to be and others' expectations don't have to define you.

5

Overcoming self-doubt and developing confidence in your teaching identity

It takes a lot of self-assuredness to question school norms and speak up for what you need. Many of us struggle with believing in our own ideas and trusting our professional judgment.

The climate in your school may be undermining your confidence, as well. You may have students and parents questioning a lot, so it feels like you're constantly defending your choices, with no one from the school backing you up.

You may feel like you have a low ability to make decisions but high accountability for the outcome of those decisions. You may be told to do something by one administrator and then given a conflicting directive by another admin, so neither of them are happy with you. You may see a misalignment between how you are evaluated and what's actually important in your job.

Institutional discrimination can increase feelings of self-doubt. If the system isn't designed to recognize the kinds of skills you bring to the table and you don't fit the typical mold of a teacher, being constantly undermined by others who doubt your expertise might leave you feeling like you're working twice as hard to be taken half as seriously. You might even internalize those feelings and wonder if you're not cut out to be a teacher, after all. This can be the case for anyone outside the dominant teacher demographic, particularly educators of color, but also people with disabilities, and even teachers who are substantially older or younger than their peers.

Any of these circumstances (and dozens more I could list) may cause you to second guess yourself.

Additionally, teaching is partially a science but also a bit of an art. That means it can never truly be standardized, quantified, or condensed into the "one correct way" ... and yet you're frequently made to feel as if there IS a right way, and it's definitely not the way you've been doing it.

You may not even know who you're *supposed* to be in the classroom, much less how to bring your whole, authentic self into the room each day. It may seem like no matter what you do, someone (whether a student, parent, or school leader) is not going to like it, and you'll feel stuck in the middle of a tug of war.

The next step in your "fewer things better" journey is to rebuild your self-confidence as an educator: to figure out your real teaching identity and step into it confidently, even when it goes against what other people expect of you.

Your true essential self — the real you, which is not acting from a place of fear, emotional wounds, unhealed trauma, defensiveness, prejudice, biases, or outside expectations — always knows the right thing to do.

Your true and essential self is *exactly* the teacher your students need.

I believe there are three components to discovering and standing strong in who you are as a teacher. We'll work on developing each of the components together in this chapter:

1) A sense of self-worth based on your inherent value as a human being (not based on how hard you work, your students' test scores, or what it says on your teaching evaluation)
2) An understanding of your own unique teaching style and how it evolves over time
3) Self-reflection skills which enable you to learn from feedback and grow, while still honoring who you are as a person and a teacher

Root out imposter syndrome

Let's start with the foundation, and tap into that sense of self-worth which has been slowly chipped away throughout the years. I'm betting some of these thoughts seem familiar:

- *I have no idea what I'm doing as a teacher.*
- *I'm not experienced enough to do this job.*
- *I'm not knowledgeable enough about this subject area to be teaching it.*
- *I'm just not capable of doing everything that needs to be done as a teacher.*
- *I don't know why other people say I'm such a good teacher — I really haven't done a very good job.*

I think almost all teachers can relate to these thoughts. And, the best educators often underestimate their abilities and focus solely on the areas they believe could be improved.

Even if your students are generally learning and engaged, parents are complimenting you, colleagues admire you, and your principal thinks you're doing a good job, you *still* might not see yourself as an effective teacher.

You might feel a bit like a fraud, and experience an almost panic-inducing sense that at any moment, other people are going to figure out you have absolutely no idea what you're doing and have no business being given the level of responsibility you have.

This is called imposter syndrome, and it can be paralyzing. If you struggle with this, you may find it's gotten worse in recent years and is exacerbated by social media, where we see (or think we're seeing) what other people's lives are like, and inadvertently begin comparing ourselves to them.

You might wonder,

How come my house or classroom doesn't look like that? How come my family or students don't act like that? Everyone else is being responsible and I still struggle with basic adulting. I can't even remember to get my teeth cleaned every six months. How am I in charge of running an entire classroom?

The way to root out imposter syndrome is by building up your sense of self-worth and learning to truly recognize your skills and accomplishments.

That's because the problem isn't other people thinking you're better than you actually are. They're not wrong about your competency.

The issue is that *they* think you're better than *you* think you are. Their view of you is higher than your view of yourself.

Imposter syndrome isn't rooted in reality or your actual skills and expertise at all. It's rooted in the way you see yourself. If you've accomplished things that are greater than your own perception of self-worth, you will experience cognitive dissonance anytime you're praised:

- *How could I be Teacher of the Year when my desk is a mess and I have 500 unread emails?*
- *Why would they want me to be team leader when I yelled at my students the other day?*
- *How could my colleagues compliment my room organization when everything inside my cabinets is a disaster?*

Because you don't measure up to some internal ideal, you don't feel like a "real adult" or maybe you just don't feel like a "real teacher."

So when others compliment your achievements and skills, it feels uncomfortable because it doesn't align with your identity. You don't see yourself as a person who could be team leader or teacher of the year or even "just" a competent classroom practitioner. You focus on all your flaws, mistakes, and limitations. Your self-image is not aligned with who you really are and what you've been able to accomplish.

It's extremely difficult to create boundaries for yourself, stand up for your needs, and be firm in what you believe if part of you feels like an imposter.

If you want to have the confidence to do fewer things better, you have to be yourself unapologetically, without letting others' expectations define you.

Getting there means understanding your strengths and knowing what you bring to the table.

Recognize the value you bring to your work each day

It can be hard to see the value of all the little tasks you do each day, because so much of the work of a teacher (like that of a parent) is mundane. It's comprised of small things that may not feel rewarding and that others don't even notice.

There's also a critic around every corner. No matter what choice you make, someone will have the opinion that you did it completely wrong. So, the only time you get feedback is when you've "messed up."

One way you can build your confidence is by choosing to notice and focus on your accomplishments. Find those small wins and celebrate the light bulb moments. Notice your own progress even when you're not yet at the goal. This will help you start to realize just how valuable *all* of your day actually is.

Do you think you spent the last 15 minutes tying shoes and zipping coats before recess?

No. You smiled at each of your students as you bundled them up to protect them from the cold. That might be just the loving, nurturing gesture some of those kids needed so they could be ready to learn from you later.

Do you think you just wasted the whole afternoon in a data chat meeting?

No. You got to step back and look at all the hard work you did compiling and analyzing information over the past month. You got to see all the evidence of just how well you know your students, and you got to learn even more information that is going to empower you to take your kids to the next level tomorrow. Who cares if someone else in the meeting made it boring or unpleasant? Look at what *you* did! Look how much more prepared you are to meet your students' needs because of the hard work you put in every day.

Do you think you just taught a developmentally inappropriate learning standard that less than half the class truly understood?

No. You helped part of the class — maybe 12 or so kids — meet an incredibly difficult objective. 12 different kids, all at the same time! And you planted a seed for the rest of the kids, who are now a few steps closer to understanding the concept when you're re-teaching tomorrow.

This is not optimistic thinking — this is realistic thinking.

It's reality. It's exactly what you did.

You show up, day after day, and work these little miracles all day long without even realizing you're doing it. You're probably so focused on everything you *didn't* do that you don't realize how much you've actually accomplished.

I am urging you — stop for a moment. Be present. Truly recognize the impact you have made.

> What you bring to the classroom is important. Ultimately, whether someone else tells you that is irrelevant. You must choose to perceive your own work as something meaningful and valuable, because it is.

Your very existence — your presence in the classroom — has value. And the more that you show up with an open heart and mind, free from limiting beliefs about yourself, your students, and your school, the more your essential self will shine through.

Think back to some moments you are most proud of as a teacher. They were probably times when you were fully present as the "real you."

During those moments, you totally immersed yourself in caring for and supporting your students, school families, or colleagues. You experienced a state of flow, where you did what you do best, in a way that comes naturally.

That's your essential self. Your true self is unburdened by to-do lists, standards, and outside expectations. It's free from unhelpful stories about what is and isn't possible. It's you in your most authentic state: present, compassionate, and filled with purpose.

To be your best self in the classroom, you don't have to become anything you are not. You don't have to strive to improve in five areas on a checklist. Focus instead on being your true, whole, healed essential self, letting go of any thoughts, beliefs, and actions that don't serve the highest good.

At your core, you are loving, patient, and kind. You are full of life and energy and purpose. All the traits that are counter to that are simply baggage and coping mechanisms you've picked up along the way in your life's journey through a very challenging world. They're reactions you've developed as a result of fear, emotional wounds, defensiveness, biases, expectations, and so on.

> *You don't have to constantly work hard to become a better teacher (or partner, or parent). You're not becoming anything. You're simply releasing all the habits and patterns that aren't actually you.*

Being yourself — your true self — is always enough. It's always exactly what's needed in any given moment.

Counter the feelings of not being or doing "enough"

Recognizing that you are enough requires a profound mindset shift in any aspect of life, but it's particularly challenging in a workplace where your competence is measured via checklist. A high-accountability system can make you feel like your value is tied up in someone else's criteria of effectiveness.

Resist the pressure to base your worth as a teacher on the results of your evaluation. If your students' test scores don't improve fast enough, that does not mean there's something wrong with you, or that you're not good enough at your job, or that you didn't work hard enough.

Your value can never be defined by the scores on a test that you didn't even take yourself.

When you feel self-doubt taking over, don't assume those thoughts about your incompetence are actually true. Anyone who strives to be their best is going to feel like an imposter at times, or worry that they don't measure up. Your concern over whether you're good enough is a sign that you care about your job. You're invested in your students' success and truly want to help them.

So, try to just observe what you're thinking and feeling. Pay attention to the events, ideas, and people who inadvertently cause you to doubt yourself or feel bad. Notice those feelings and tell yourself:

> *Something in this situation is triggering feelings of self-doubt. I'm feeling a bit like a fraud right now, and questioning whether I'm good enough for this job.*
>
> *But just because I'm thinking and feeling this way at the moment doesn't mean that my doubts are reality or that I need to give any consideration or credence to them.*
>
> *I'm just going to observe that it's happening, and let those thoughts and feelings pass on their own. They always do!*
>
> *I know deep inside that I am enough, and my efforts are enough. And, I am getting more skilled and experienced at my job over time.*

The only thing I need to focus on is showing up as my essential self. My true self is just the person my students need, and that's the very best job I can do.

Your belief that you are enough has to be independent of whether everyone else thinks you're enough. As the saying goes, you could be the sweetest peach in the orchard, but there's still going to be somebody who doesn't like peaches.

Some administrators will watch your best lesson and be unimpressed. Some students and parents will dislike you, no matter what.

Some of your colleagues will disagree with the way you manage your classroom and teach your lessons. There are people who will look at how you set up your beautifully organized classroom and think, *Meh, not my style.*

Your sense of self-worth does not have to be shaken by this. Their opinions and evaluations are subjective, and not an accurate measure of everything you bring to the classroom.

Try to be open to the critique, and self-reflect:

- How can you use their feedback to your benefit as an opportunity for growth?
- What's the grain of truth in what the person's saying that is worth holding onto, even while you disregard the part that isn't helpful?
- Do you have a solid rationale for WHY you're making the choices you're making? (If so, practice articulating it; if not, dig deeper to uncover whether your choice was the right one, or if this is an opportunity to go in a different direction.)

Asking yourself these questions will help you use other people's opinions and evaluations as a springboard for more insight into yourself. Use these questions to help you evaluate your growth in a way that is useful for self-improvement, rather than working to please others or measure up to some arbitrary standard.

Let go of "one right way" pressure and let your identity evolve

Believing in the effectiveness of your own unique teaching style is an important part of doing fewer things better. It gives you the confidence to say no and ditch the stuff that's inauthentic and unhelpful to you, even if your path looks different than everyone else's.

There's no "right way" to teach or manage a classroom, because there's no singular approach that is effective for every student.

There's also no method that every teacher can authentically pull off.

You might compose an original song to teach a concept and stand on the table to dance, but I'd feel ridiculous if I tried to emulate that. It wouldn't work for my personality, and therefore, it wouldn't be the best approach for my students. They'd probably be cringing or laughing the whole time.

The solution isn't for me to get more comfortable with singing and dancing. Nor is the solution to force the people who are natural performers to be more subdued.

Being true to who you are is an essential part of uncovering your most effective teaching style.

You can be an awesome teacher whether you're high energy or low key, silly or serious, extroverted or introverted. Embracing your natural preferences and personality traits will allow you to stop putting on an act of what you think a teacher "should" be like, and connect authentically with students instead.

While I think most folks would agree there's no "right way" in theory, the reality is that being yourself will not necessarily allow you to fit in and meet expectations at your school. Each school's culture will place more value on certain teaching styles over others.

Some of this is related to demographics and location. What's effective for kindergarten in rural Montana is not what's effective for high school in uptown Manhattan. But school culture is also influenced by the values of the community, school leadership, and veteran staff members.

For example, one school might encourage frequent use of technology, while another might actively minimize students' screen time.

If you feel passionately about one approach and teach in a school with opposite values, you'll have to compromise and step out of your comfort zone more often. You'll also have to accept that you're the odd one out, and choose to connect with like-minded teachers in other settings so you can feel supported. You'll need to ground yourself in the research behind your approach so that you won't be constantly second-guessing your lessons or feel unprepared to defend them.

If your approach doesn't seem to be working or you can't manage to meet expectations, you might not be doing something "wrong." Maybe you just haven't found a school where your teaching philosophy is effective and valued.

While it's not always easy, the happiest educators I know are those who prioritized finding a school that is aligned with their methodologies. I see far too many teachers burn out and assume the problem is the whole profession, rather than just a conflict with their district or school or perhaps even a single administrator.

The way that morale and school culture varies from one building to another — even within the same zip code — is extraordinary to witness. If you love teaching, it is worth the effort to find a school where you can thrive.

Of course, figuring out who you are (as a person and teacher) and finding a school that's aligned with your values is basically the journey of a lifetime. It's likely that you won't really know who you are as a teacher for many years, and you might not ever teach in a "perfect fit" school (though a good fit can be enough to give you the freedom to interact with kids in a way that feels natural).

I also think age has a huge impact on our teaching styles, and our preferences and interests shift a lot as we grow older. I certainly was not the same kind of teacher when I started at age 21 as I was at age 31, and I'd be a very different teacher today. Not only had I changed over the course of a decade, but so did our schools, and so did the world.

Your identity as a teacher will (and should) evolve constantly as you learn from experiences, new research, and personal and professional development.

 YOUR TEACHING STYLE IS NOT SOMETHING YOU HAVE TO FIGURE OUT ONCE AND FOR ALL, THEN STICK TO FOREVER. TRIAL AND ERROR IS REQUIRED TO DISCOVER THE "SPECIAL SAUCE" THAT YOU ALONE CAN BRING TO THE CLASSROOM, AND YOU HAVE TO KEEP EXPERIMENTING WITH IT OVER THE COURSE OF YOUR CAREER.

It's important to view your identity (teacher, dad, wife, etc.) as something that will change over time. If you are too entrenched in your identity ("I will never do X" or "I'm the type of teacher who will always do Y"), then it becomes difficult to consider information which conflicts with that belief about yourself. Experimenting with a more efficient or effective approach will require you to change your entire self-image.

Choose instead to build your self-image on the idea of having a growth mindset — of being a person who is always changing, learning, and improving over time. That way you won't feel like you have to do things the way you've always done them, or place judgments or labels on your past choices.

Even when you were clearly wrong in the past, you don't have to get stuck in shame and guilt. We all have regrets about things we've done in the classroom. If you didn't feel like you'd made mistakes, that wouldn't mean you were perfect. It would mean you're not growing or reflecting on your practice.

It's impossible for a self-reflective person to look back at their teaching career and feel like they did everything right. Keep moving forward, and do the best you know how in any given moment.

Allow other teachers to inspire you instead of comparing yourself

Part of the way you develop confidence in your teaching style and allow it to evolve over time is by learning from other teachers and experimenting with their practices.

And throughout this process, you'll probably compare yourself to those other teachers. It's a natural reaction.

You might see coworkers who let students hang out with them after school, and wonder if you're not doing a good enough job at building relationships and offering support to students.

You might watch teachers who are super laidback and friendly with kids, and assume you need to lighten up and stop being so strict.

Or maybe you'll see teachers who never seem to have fun with their students but get high test scores, and wonder if you should abandon all the memorable experiences you give your students and get down to business more often.

You won't be able to avoid this self-doubt altogether, but you can honor it, because questioning helps you reflect on your practice. Use it to help you grow, rather than bowing to the pressure to blindly emulate the most effective teachers in your school or district.

You're not them, and if you try to be, the best outcome you can hope for is to be a mediocre copy. It's far more effective (and sustainable) to be the best version of yourself.

THE GOAL IS TO ALLOW OTHER TEACHERS TO BE AN INSPIRATION TO YOU, RATHER THAN AN IDEAL WHICH YOU COMPARE YOURSELF TO AND TRY TO BECOME.

EMULATING OTHERS TOO MUCH OR PAYING TOO MUCH ATTENTION TO WHAT THEY'RE DOING WILL CAUSE YOU TO FALL INTO A COMPARISON TRAP WHICH CREATES MORE SELF-DOUBT.

That means you need to filter the things you learn from other teachers through the lens of what makes sense for you right now in your current teaching context. You don't have to do everything they're doing, and you don't have to do it all right now!

Also remember that just because a practice is admired in your school, that doesn't mean it's best for teachers or kids. What's normal or accepted is not necessarily what's healthy. Be cautious not to mindlessly adapt your teaching philosophy to match the norms of the school.

For example, I once taught in an elementary school where the norm was to let kids run wild in the hallways. Students were constantly shouting, stomping, and making it impossible for the other classes to learn, even with our doors closed.

I was the only one in our hallway who required students to walk quietly. My kids would ask me, "How come we have to be quiet and they don't?" The pressure to conform was real, and there were many days when I wondered if I should change my rules to match what everyone else was doing.

But I knew that wasn't going to work for *me*.

I needed my students to be calm in the hallways so they could enter the classroom quietly and get to work right away. I couldn't let them yell and run, and then two seconds later get them to sit down and focus.

I did some self-reflection and discussed the issue with a couple friends I respected, fully expecting them to agree the norms in my school were "wrong" and my way was "right."

But through those conversations, I realized my approach was a bit reminiscent of a chain gang. I didn't want any part of my classroom management to resemble prison procedures, and I decided to make some changes.

I stopped requiring students to be completely silent in the hall and hold their hands in a specific position. My kids deserved a bit more freedom, and I was willing to try a different way.

As it turned out, they were able to handle less strictness in the hallway while still respecting the rights of other students who were trying to learn.

It may have taken me much longer to figure that out and be willing to change my expectations if the school norm hadn't prompted me to think through my philosophy more deeply.

Idealizing other teachers or blindly copying them doesn't work. Neither does entrenching ourselves deeply in our separate camps, pitting ourselves against one another's "wrong" approaches.

Through the process of comparing yourself to other teachers, you can uncover aspects of their practice which you can take inspiration or learn from. You can then experiment with ways to take a piece of their approach that's useful and incorporate it into your teaching style.

Self-reflect to find an approach in "the green zone"

On one side of the spectrum, we have teaching styles that are so lenient it creates chaos and interferes with student learning, and on the other side, we have styles that are so strict they destroy children's sense of worth and create a deeply uncomfortable learning environment.

I think of those extremes as "red zones."

But for most teachers, most of the time, the choices we make in the classroom do not fall on total opposite ends of the spectrum.

There is a huge area in the middle (a "green zone") where you can choose among many viable options, and you can develop the confidence in yourself to figure out where you stand and feel good about it.

I encourage you to evaluate the way you are running your classroom and be honest with yourself about how well it's meeting the needs of your students.

Consider not just the measurable outcomes, but how those choices make you feel and how they make your students feel. As Maya Angelou stated, "People will forget what you said. People will forget what you did. But people will never forget how you made them feel."

I think that should be our guiding principle as we uncover our own unique teaching styles and philosophies. It's less about having perfect lessons and flawless classroom procedures, and more about how we make kids feel.

Do they know we believe in them?

Have we helped them develop confidence in their own worth, abilities, and identities?

Do they leave our classrooms feeling empowered and prepared to advocate for themselves?

Are we offering them a sense of agency, and supporting them in their goals instead of conforming them to ours?

These are the kinds of things that matter ... and you can accomplish them by being a bubbly cheerleader-type of teacher, or a quiet wise mentor. You might be a stern father figure, a fun big sis, a loving grandmother, or someone who defies labels altogether. Show up for the kids as your essential self — whatever that looks like for you.

Stay true to yourself as you continually reflect on your instructional and classroom management choices. Be prepared to shed the old approaches that don't work for you or your students anymore.

Remember that self-reflection is what differentiates the truly effective teacher, and the core of your identity has to be a willingness to grow. Choose to view yourself as a person who is adaptable and open to new ideas. Notice:

- Are you taking the time to evaluate what is actually working for you and your kids?
- Are you directly confronting your shortcomings and looking for a better way?
- Are you staying open to learning from other people and using what they've learned as an inspiration for you to keep growing?

Because while there's no one right way to teach, there *are* some ineffective ways, and we will all have lapses in judgment at times.

You can be the most amazing, experienced teacher, and you'll still make mistakes in the classroom. You can love your students like your own and still have implicit biases toward them. You can feel like you're crushing it with a certain teaching strategy and have total blind spots about the long-term impact on your students.

I believe we need to create a culture in education in which we are open to self-reflection and can challenge one another to be our best. We need to embrace conversations about what's good for kids and why we've made the choices we have in our classrooms.

We can't get defensive and insist everyone should just do whatever they think is best. We need to recondition ourselves to see critical thinking as a positive thing because it helps us become better in our work.

Choose an accountability partner to help you grow your confidence

I encourage you to find a person you can partner up with to ensure you are having *real and honest* conversations about your practice. Choose someone whose opinions and perspective you respect: someone who's an outstanding teacher, does great things for kids, and gives you sound advice.

This is going to be the person you can ask: *Did I make the right choice here? Should I do something different? Is this really working? Do I need to change some things in this area?*

Pick a person you trust to be honest with you and give you solid feedback in a supportive, constructive way, and offer to do the same thing for them.

Together, make the commitment to continually:

- Question the status quo
- Move out of your comfort zones
- Converse about what's best for kids
- Ask questions about how you can improve
- Build true camaraderie beyond surface-level support
- Have honest dialogue about your strengths and weaknesses
- Receive feedback with curiosity rather than defensiveness
- Self-examine beyond intent and question your impact
- Challenge one another to be your best.

You can download a printable copy of this agreement at FTBproject.com.

When you are grounded firmly in the *why* behind your choices and are honest with yourself about the areas you need to grow in, you don't have to base your self-worth on whether everyone approves of and is impressed with your work.

When you decide that you are who you want to be and others' expectations don't define you, you'll start to feel you don't have to defend yourself or change other people's minds.

You'll begin to base your instructional decisions on what's truly best for kids, and understand clearly what you need to keep doing and what you can remove from your workload.

You'll begin to set your own expectations, and define the role of teacher for yourself, so that no one else can control the narrative.

6

Defining expectations for yourself and creating healthy boundaries

Just as you can question school norms, you can also question the norms that school has created in your time apart from work. In fact, you can question *all* norms that impact the quality of your life.

You get to design your own lifestyle, in the sense that you can decide where to focus your attention and energy. You get to choose many of your daily routines, and decide how a good portion of your time is spent.

For instance, you can expose yourself to every person's random opinions by scrolling through social media endlessly each evening, or read a book by a person whose ideas are wise and helpful for you.

You can flip aimlessly through TV channels and watch 3 minutes of 10 different programs, or fill your watchlist queue with things that you know will be interesting or uplifting.

You can let the weekend slip away on mundane tasks, or devote a couple hours to an art class at the community center, going to a museum, playing with your nieces and nephews, participating in a softball league, or hiking on local trails.

Regularly choosing any of these activities makes them a part of your lifestyle, and there are countless different lifestyle possibilities.

Of course, there can be circumstances which undermine your quality of life and are not within your control. I'm not saying you can choose everything about how you experience life. Some negative circumstances aren't easily changed, and that can have a big impact on how much time you spend in a natural state of contentment.

However, you can choose more than you may recognize, and poor circumstances don't condemn you to a miserable life.

Your life circumstances are not synonymous with your lifestyle.

We've all heard of celebrities who have an enviable lifestyle yet are tragically unhappy, and we've all known people living ordinary lives but seem to glow from the inside. So, experiencing a high quality of life isn't necessarily about having a lot of money or free time or living in a beautiful location.

 THE QUALITY OF YOUR LIFE IS MOST DEEPLY IMPACTED BY THE INTENTIONALITY OF YOUR DAILY ROUTINES AND RITUALS. IT'S AN ALIGNMENT BETWEEN THE THINGS YOU FOCUS ON WITH THE THINGS YOU WANT TO BE FOCUSING ON.

You can choose a lifestyle that is fulfilling and full of joy, or miserable and depressing (sometimes without changing a single circumstance, and only altering your mindset and habits).

So, what does a fulfilling lifestyle look like for you?

What qualities in yourself and gifts do you want to nurture and utilize?

How do you want to be spending your time?

Maybe these are questions you've never asked yourself before. Or maybe this is something you decided in a different season of life, and now it's time to re-evaluate.

The truth is that you can be whoever you want to be. You can focus your time and attention wherever you to want to focus them. Let's examine how to take charge of your daily habits and create boundaries.

Redefine "normal" in a way that works for YOU

So much of how we experience life gets chalked up to, "Ah, what are you gonna do? That's just the way it is." But we often lose sight of how much of our daily life is influenced by cultural standards.

As Manny Scott once said, "Your cultural universe is not culturally universal."

Almost every obligation in your day is a reflection of the time and place you are located, and the people you have surrounded yourself with. It's not the only way to live.

For example, I have a friend who feels run ragged by driving her three kids around to all their activities. She spends more than two hours a day in the car, and hates every minute of it. When I asked why she doesn't make some changes to the way her household is run, she indicated it doesn't feel like a choice: "It's just what I need to do for my family right now."

But let's take a step back here, and examine this through a wider lens.

Spending 10-12 hours a week dropping off and picking up kids from dance and soccer practice is a 21st century American conception of how a mom is obligated to spend her time. It's a cultural construct, established primarily for middle class white suburban moms, but which impacts expectations for other races and socio-economic groups, as well.

It's not universal. This wasn't always our norm. And, there are still millions of people all over the world who do not spend hours each week playing chauffeur for their children.

I know parents here in the U.S. who live in rural areas where there aren't a lot of extracurricular activities, and their kids spend most of their free time doing things around the house with family.

I know parents who live in urban areas where many activities are within walking distance, and kids are taught how to move around the city together in groups via public transportation.

And, I know parents in suburban areas where constant chauffeuring is seen as unavoidable, and yet they choose to say,

"That's not how our family is going to operate. Each child picks ONE activity, and that's it. The majority of our time is going to be spent together at home, not racing from one event to another. I'm going to arrange a carpool with other parents so I'm only responsible for pick up and drop off once a week. Just because crazy busy is normal for everyone else, doesn't mean that's going to be normal for us."

 SINCE YOUR CULTURAL UNIVERSE IS NOT CULTURALLY UNIVERSAL, YOU DON'T HAVE TO LET WHAT YOU SEE AROUND YOU LIMIT THE POSSIBILITIES FOR WHAT YOUR LIFE COULD BE LIKE.

Think for a moment about who you're letting set the tone for what's normal or ideal. Do they seem to be fulfilled? Are they content with how their time is spent?

What are the hidden sacrifices they're making? Are you willing to do what they're doing to have what they have?

And most importantly — do you really WANT a life that resembles theirs? Would it work for YOU and the people you care about?

Almost every person I know wishes they had more control over how they use their time, and I'm guessing the same is true for the people you know. So, don't look to other folks to set the standard.

Dream bigger than what you see. Imagine better possibilities and allow your mind to wander to unconventional solutions.

When you recognize "normal" as nothing more than a cultural construct that's currently dominant in your area, you can reinvent your life to prioritize things that matter to *you*.

Notice how judgment keeps you from seeing new possibilities

You might be thinking, *That sounds great in theory … but what will people say about me or our family?* Maybe you're imagining the worst impressions people would have if you dare to be different.

I've struggled with this quite a bit myself, but I've noticed that it gets better with age. I naturally care less about other people's opinions as I grow older. Plus, carving out your own path takes less effort once you've spent years clearing the way and establishing the road you want.

I've also observed which habits make it harder for me to design the life I want. The more I immerse myself in what other people are doing (especially if I'm judging or being critical of their choices), the harder it is for me to feel confident in my own choices.

If I spend time gossiping or scrolling through social media while thinking judgmental thoughts about what I see, that increases my self-doubt and people-pleasing tendency. The next time I need to break with convention, my mind repeats all those same things I was thinking or reading online.

I start worrying: *If I was watching other people and thinking critical thoughts about them, surely others are watching my every move and thinking critical thoughts about me!*

These concerns are minimized, though, when I spend less time talking about other people, limit my time on social media, and share fewer aspects of my personal life online.

Being mindful in these areas helps me avoid placing undue focus on what other people are thinking, doing, wearing, eating, watching, and so on. And, I'm not opening up my life choices for the scrutiny of strangers and random acquaintances. As the saying goes, their opinions about me are none of my business.

The less concerned you are about the choices other people make, the easier it will be to show yourself grace and non-judgment. You'll be less likely to get caught up in all the terrible things other people might think about your life choices, because those kind of judgmental thoughts won't already be circling around in your mind.

In other words, when you stop expecting other people to live in a way that pleases you, you won't feel so obligated to live in a way that pleases other people.

My friend Dan Tricarico of the Zen Teacher Project has practiced asking himself, "What is the most generous assumption I can make?" and thinking that through when he finds himself being judgmental. The self-talk might go something like this:

> My natural inclination is to label this person as rude (or weird or ignorant or lazy). But what's the most generous assumption I can

make? What else might be true here that I haven't considered? What's a more compassionate way to see the situation?

Notice how much energy you are expending mocking other people's choices. For example, are you questioning how your students' families spend their money, or scoffing at their living arrangements? Are you snickering at the names they've given their children, rolling your eyes at their outfits, or making assumptions about how little they must care about education?

Indulging yourself in these kinds of thoughts and conversations is toxic to your sense of well-being. Not only does it poison your relationships with families — who can likely sense your judgmental attitude — you're also poisoning your own mind.

If you recognize yourself in this pattern, please know that breaking it can be one of the most powerful takeaways you get from this book. An addiction to gossip and judgmental tendencies may be holding you back in ways that only become clear in hindsight.

Anytime you become too focused on arbitrary standards for what people (including yourself) "ought to do," you're creating frustration. There is no one single way to live life which will make everyone happy, or that will please everyone else.

So, spend less time thinking about other people's choices and opinions, make the most generous assumption about them, and focus on living the life *you* want.

How to figure out what you want more (and less of) in your life

If you don't yet know (or haven't had the mental bandwidth to think about) what you want your life to look like and how you want to spend your time, the key to getting started is simple.

It's all about mindfulness. As you go about your regular daily routines, notice how you feel.

Let's say you spend an hour exercising. How do you feel when you make that choice? Is it a habit that's worth keeping? Is it producing results you want?

Pay attention to the parts of that choice that you like and don't like. Do you enjoy the workout but hate the drive to the gym? Do you like how you feel after the workout, but dislike sweating and feeling overheated?

Tuning in to what you like helps you figure out which elements to keep and what you might want to eliminate. Maybe going for a walk or jog around your neighborhood could give you a break from commuting to the gym. Or, maybe swimming or doing yoga on occasion could allow you to move physically but not be dripping with sweat.

Also, notice how you feel on the days when you don't exercise. Do you have more or less energy on those days? How would it feel to take more days off from working out? How would it feel to add more days in?

Don't be afraid to experiment — that's how you'll discover what really works for you!

The idea is to train yourself to be in tune with how you're feeling physically, emotionally, and spiritually each day. Start to identify how your different routines are creating the life you want to live (so you can do more of those things) and how your routines are hindering you (so you can try alternative options).

How does it feel when you've spent a half hour playing with your kids or pet? What aspects of that experience were tiring? Which were most enjoyable? Could you experiment with ways to make that time even more fulfilling?

How does it feel when you've spent an hour watching TV? Do you notice that sometimes it's relaxing and fun, and other times, it feels like a waste of time and you wish you'd gotten off the couch? Pay attention to this — notice the times of day, types of programs, and other circumstances that make TV feel good and the ones that make TV feel bad.

How does it feel when you take a few minutes at night to care for your teeth, skin, and hair? What if you listen to an audiobook or relaxing music during that routine? How does that feel different than when you're frantically trying to multitask at the same time, or cutting those routines short because you just want to collapse into bed?

There's nothing in your daily habits that should be above questioning, including what happens at school. Just because everyone else on your team eats lunch together doesn't mean you have to. What feeds your soul? What is nourishing to you? You can eat alone in your room and meditate for the last five minutes of your break. You can go for a walk around the perimeter of campus and listen to energizing music while you get fresh air. You can video chat with a friend who makes you laugh and helps you put work problems in perspective.

Your time and focus are your own. Only you can make these decisions about where to expend your energy.

As you start training yourself to think in this way, it's important to enter the process without judgment. Don't label your choices as "good" or "bad" or indulge in feelings of guilt over how you spent your time.

Just go through your regular daily routines, and observe how you feel during each element. What is giving you energy? What is draining your energy? The simple act of bringing awareness to your habits will help you be in tune with your wants and needs, so you can make more intentional choices in the future.

Winners DO quit; they just quit the right things at the right time

Observing which routines and habits feel good and which don't will help you make a natural progression toward doing fewer things better. You'll get the first inkling of things you'd like to let go of.

For example, you might notice that:

- Hitting the alarm eight times and then rushing around sets a frantic tone to your day, and you want to give yourself a few minutes to get centered
- Watching the news for too long makes you depressed, and you want to skim the headlines online instead
- Going to a colleague's room to gossip after school is de-energizing and causes you to stay late, so you want to only hang out once a week
- Spending every evening hustling to various activities makes it hard to get to bed on time, so you want to quit a social commitment and have an evening for settling in with a puzzle or book

Almost any habit which is draining your energy or stressing you out can be restructured so that it feels at least a little bit better. And, when you're truly aware of the detrimental effects and not just rushing mindlessly through your day, it becomes much easier to let go of unhealthy habits.

Even though these seem like little things, you may need to explicitly give yourself permission to change here. Often our identities are wrapped up in the way we do life.

We can't see ourselves getting up earlier because we don't believe we're morning people, or we can't imagine not serving on the community board because we see ourselves as informed neighbors. We can't imagine quitting the bowling league even though it stopped being fun years ago, because we see ourselves as social butterflies who always go out on Saturday night.

Whatever the situation might be, give yourself space to grow as a person, just as you're giving yourself space to grow as an educator.

 NEVER BE AFRAID OF CANCELLING, CHANGING, OR QUITTING SOMETHING THAT IS NO LONGER SERVING YOU WELL. IT IS NOT A FAILURE TO ADMIT THAT SOMETHING YOU USED TO DO ISN'T THE BEST USE OF YOUR TIME NOW.

It takes awhile to internalize this mindset, because it directly contradicts the advice we've been given from a young age:

Never give up.
Only losers quit.
When you quit, you've lost.
The only failure is in giving up.

But as Seth Godin once noted, successful people quit all the time; they simply quit the right things at the right time.

That's certainly been true for me. I've quit tons of things in my life: committees, grading practices, Facebook groups, social commitments, holiday traditions, vacation plans, friendships … honestly, the list is endless.

And not all of those things were awful. Many were working fairly well, but I had to make tough choices, because there wasn't enough room in my life to do them all.

I had to let go of the good to make time for the great.

Quitting doesn't mean admitting defeat or that you were wasting your time previously. It doesn't undermine how important that thing was at an earlier time in your life, and it doesn't have to mean you'll never pick it back up again.

It just means that something isn't right for you at this moment. Don't be afraid to cut your losses and walk away.

Create boundaries, not ultimatums

Some of the things you'll want to quit doing or change might require you to create new boundaries with other people.

There are a lot of misconceptions about boundaries, and often they're confused with ultimatums. However, creating a boundary does not mean telling your partner or colleagues, "I'm not doing this by myself anymore and you're going to help me!"

Boundaries are not things you try to force other people to do. Since you can't control anyone's behavior but your own, you can't create a boundary that will only be effective if other people change.

Brooke Castillo teaches that a proper boundary is an action you take to protect yourself, not control other people, and it must be based on your own actions: *If X happens, I will do Y.*

For example, let's say you've been noticing how stressful it feels when students' parents contact you on the weekend. You've realized you jump every time the phone rings, and can't relax because you feel pressure to check your email every few hours. The stress of not knowing what kind of message you might be dealing with at 11 p.m. on a Saturday night has become too much.

You might decide you are no longer going to respond to emails on the weekend to protect your time and well-being. The boundary you create should be based on what YOU will do if parents email or call.

You might send a message to all parents which reads, "You can email me anytime it's convenient for you. I will read the message and respond to you between the hours of 8 a.m. and 5 p.m., Monday-Friday." Then, if you receive an email over the weekend, you must enforce your own boundary, and wait until Monday morning to reply.

Here's another example. Maybe you've been noticing that coworkers wander into your room during your planning period, and it's preventing you from getting any work done. Your boundary must be based on what YOU will do if they come into your room while you're working.

Say to them, "I'm setting aside my planning period so I can have uninterrupted time to grade papers. I really need that time because it's the only chance I have during the school day. If you come by in the morning, I can be available. But if you come by during my planning period, the door will be locked so I can get this grading knocked out and get home at a reasonable hour." Then keep the door locked every day, just as you stated.

If that feels harsh to you, remind yourself that school is your workplace. You are a professional, and have no need to apologize for behaving like one. Nurturing friendships with colleagues is fine sometimes, but it should be considered reasonable to close the door and focus on work. You are paid to be a teacher to your students, and that's your top priority, not protecting the feelings of your colleagues who might be hurt if you don't hang around and chat.

As you can tell, *setting* boundaries is fairly easy, but *following through* with them is much harder. When you create a boundary, you must be prepared to communicate it clearly, and stick to it.

Remind yourself that you are entitled to create a boundary if it helps you do your job more effectively, protects your time, or allows you to take better care of yourself.

Just remember that you cannot expect others to change in response to your boundaries. Expecting their behavior to be different will create frustration and strained relationships. So if the boundary is that you will not be attending any new extracurricular events, explain that, and stop agreeing to participate! But don't expect people to stop asking you. The boundary is that YOU will say no.

When creating boundaries exacts too high a price

I know the idea of saying no and setting boundaries feels very empowering.

But I have to be honest: There will be instances in which you can't set the boundaries you need without paying dearly.

This is true about household and family obligations, but particularly true in the workplace where there may be more factors that are out of your control.

Here's what I mean.

I know a teacher — let's call her Keisha — who started a position as a media specialist last year. She was dismayed to find that she didn't have a desk or chair to sit at. There was no place to put her personal belongings, and the only furniture around was student seating and bookshelves. The computer and scanner to check out books were resting on the floor.

Keisha spent the first three hours on her new job just scrounging for a desk and chair. She finally located one that was at least 40 years old with two drawers that were permanently locked, and a chair that was broken and squeaky. She considered not having a desk or chair at all, but frankly that felt like even more of an indignity — to not have a single space in the entire room which could be hers while she assisted kids in checking out books.

Just as the custodian moved the desk in for her, a colleague who worked with small groups in the back of the media center stormed in and said she had been planning to use the desk. She was furious it was moved. She had talked to the principal about it, and the principal indicated they should share the desk.

Meaning, there were two working drawers, and each teacher should use one while taking turns sitting at the desk.

These are the indignities of teaching that are incomprehensible if you have not worked in a school yourself. You have no ability to even conceive of this sort of treatment when you first enter the profession, and the toll it takes on you can be massive.

It's incredibly demoralizing when no one in your organization ever has the resources they need, and everyone's fighting amongst each other for scraps. Over the years we internalize this scarcity mindset and learn to constantly settle for less than we deserve.

And yet, what could Keisha really do in this situation? What boundary could she set? It wasn't her desk, and she had no more right to it than the other teacher. She could spend her own money to buy something more suitable, or make do.

This is the perpetual dilemma of a teacher:

Do I take the financial hit, or deal with the time and mental cost of always having to "make do" with inadequate resources?

In teaching, you will not always be able to set proper boundaries. There will be times when people are disrespectful to you, and you cannot cut them out of your life because it's your job to support them. Working conditions will at times be dirty, uncomfortable, or even unhealthy. And though these issues are more pervasive in certain schools than others, some indignities are just inherent to the job.

You can always choose to leave, and you can always choose to fight for better working conditions. I think I've made that clear throughout this book. But if you choose to stay and tolerate it, that can be an honorable decision, as well.

Do you know why Keisha is choosing to stay at a school where she wasn't even given a desk? She really, really wants to make a difference for the kids in her building.

She attended that very school as a student, and believes strongly in the nature of the work she was hired to do. The indignities of the job are a worthwhile sacrifice to her, because she has a powerful vision for what she hopes to accomplish there as a media specialist. She wants to use books the way Rudine Sims Bishop described them: as "windows, mirrors, and sliding glass doors" to help kids see a reflection of themselves and a glimpse into new worlds and possibilities.

The decision to choose the indignities in teaching is not dissimilar to choosing them in parenting. As a mom or dad, you willingly subject yourself to sleepless nights, dirty diapers, and all the mundane and repetitive drudgery of raising small humans. But some of the time (perhaps even most of the time, depending on your personality), those things won't feel like too heavy a burden, because the desire to have a family makes it worthwhile. The love you have for your children and your vision for their future makes all the hardship feel like a reasonable trade off.

If you choose to be committed to a school in which the work comes at a great personal cost, I think that's commendable. I don't believe that level of self-sacrifice is required or necessary in order to make a difference in the world. And, I don't think you are obligated to stay in that situation for years. You do not have to tolerate poor working conditions to prove your dedication to kids or the profession.

But you may choose to stay in a particular school because it feels like the right place for you to be right now (or the best choice among a limited set of options).

Simply be aware of the toll this takes on you and your loved ones, rather than trying to be a superhero or savior. Make sure you're not neglecting your own needs until you experience a breakdown.

Accept the indignities of teaching for the love of the work

When there's some aspect of your workload that you hate tolerating but know you need to because it's your best option for now, use these five strategies to help you cope.

1) Practice radical acceptance

Getting real about what teaching involves in your school is crucial. Don't keep repeating to yourself, *This is unbelievable; I can't believe I have to deal with this.* It's happening, so believe it. Subjecting yourself to these indignities is something you are *choosing* to do, as no one can stop you from quitting. You can apply for other jobs or take constructive steps to improve working conditions, but do so while practicing radical acceptance of your current reality.

Radical acceptance is a psychology term coined by Marsha Linehan and rooted in ancient Buddhist teachings. It doesn't mean you approve of your problems or deem them as okay. Radical acceptance is about avoiding unnecessary suffering by accepting rather than resisting what is. You need all your strength to teach, and practicing radical acceptance will keep you from wasting energy on perpetual outrage.

2) Refocus on a clear purpose that makes those indignities worthwhile

Some teachers care deeply about the community or population they serve; others want to share their love of their subject matter; and still others want to be the mentor and role model they had (or wish they'd had) themselves in their youth.

You may choose to stay in your school as a "martyr for the cause" due to a deep passion for equity and justice within the educational system. This is very different from having *martyr syndrome*, where you're working unnecessarily to prove your own worth and dedication or to get admiration from others.

Choosing to sacrifice your own needs and tolerate discomfort to make a difference is a worthwhile endeavor. But you must believe strongly in that mission and surround yourself with like-minded people in order to withstand the more demeaning and difficult tasks. The more clearly you can see and focus on your vision, the less draining your job will feel.

3) Exercise autonomy whenever possible

Find all the aspects of your instruction, routines, policies, and daily schedule for which you have some decision-making power, and exercise it. Often we spend far too much energy on things that are out of our control, and we miss the aspects we're able to influence. The elements of your day where you have some choice can be used in ways that re-energize you, so don't let them slip away. Look for small ways you can have more autonomy.

4) Be mindful of boundaries in your personal life so that you don't feel constantly violated at work AND at home

If you feel taken advantage of and disrespected all day long at work, it's imperative that you don't allow that after school, too. Examine your lifestyle choices, and question cultural norms which limit your agency and drain your time. Be aware of the toll that work is taking, and minimize responsibilities and obligations apart from work as much as possible. It's okay to do that for a season of your life. Recognize the amount of energy you are spending on serving and supporting others at school, and don't pressure yourself to do so in excessive levels elsewhere.

5) Incorporate daily self-care habits and rituals

Working in a school with low morale or an unhealthy environment can have far-reaching negative effects on us, and so can the impact of trauma that kids are carrying into our classrooms. Adding rituals to your day which help you refocus and decompress will make a huge difference. We'll explore specific habits for self-care in the final chapter of this book. But for now, look for small moments you can take for yourself during morning routines and breaks, and purposefully add elements to the school day which are rejuvenating and uplifting.

Part Three

I KNOW WHAT'S IMPORTANT AND ALLOCATE TIME ACCORDINGLY

"Carla" is a friend who gave me permission to share her story here. Her dream is to conduct professional development and give teacher workshops as a side hustle for now, and then take an early retirement from the classroom to do consulting full time.

She was recently invited to speak for a neighboring district on a topic she is well-known for within her school. The opportunity was a huge boost to her resume, and given her career objectives, saying yes was a no-brainer. Because she was so knowledgeable about the topic and had presented on it previously, preparation would've probably taken her no more than half an hour.

When I asked her how the event had gone, she told me she'd decided not to do it after all. Her grandmother was visiting that week, she was behind on grading, and she felt like she just had too many things going on.

I was baffled by this choice. Certainly, time with her grandmother was important, but the event would take two hours out of her day. It was so well-matched with her life goals that it would be worth the investment of time. She could have skipped the gym, an errand, an appointment, or anything else planned which wasn't a rare and special opportunity, and focus on her grandmother and this speaking event.

But in Carla's mind at the time, her decision was justified. Her grandmother was important to her — family before work, right? Why spread yourself too thin?

Through our conversation later, it became clear that Carla didn't really decline the event because she was worried about spending two hours away f r o m her grandmother. Her grandmother would have been proud of Carla's accomplishments, and probably would have wanted to watch her speak.

This wasn't about her grandmother at all. It was self-sabotage.

Staying perpetually busy and overcommitted is a common way people hold themselves back from fulfilling their dreams.

When you're constantly in motion, you have an excuse for delaying your goals: *I can't right now because I have to do this thing first, and then I have to take care of that thing, plus there's 472 other things I'm doing right now. Maybe one day I'll get to it.*

In that line of thinking, the goal seems justifiably delayed. But "one day" never comes, because you keep filling up your schedule with more things, every single day.

Carla realized afterward that she had allowed her short-term obligations to cloud her long-term vision. She had identified a goal she wanted to accomplish for her life, career, and financial stability, and yet she wasn't able to make choices about her time which were aligned with that goal.

She knew what she wanted, but wasn't managing her time in a way to help her get it.

Without even realizing it was happening — or why she was allowing it — Carla permitted other obligations to take over every moment of the day. She didn't have time to think about big picture stuff, which meant she didn't have to face the reality that her big goals were never going to happen if she didn't intentionally create change.

By staying busy with everyday tasks, Carla didn't have to make decisions. The lack of margin in her schedule made the decision for her.

So when a big opportunity came up, she didn't have any flexibility to shift things around in her schedule to accommodate it. This created an easy "out."

Doing the presentation was going to require more time, energy, and focus than she had to give. And that's the ultimate consequence when we choose to overschedule ourselves: it's not just the *time* we lack for what matters most.

It's the *ability to show up the way we need to for the things we care about*.

You've been there, too, right? Maybe you've cooked an elaborate holiday meal that left you too exhausted and cranky to make proper memories with the family. (I'm guilty — I snapped at everyone that Thanksgiving and couldn't wait until it was over.)

Or maybe you worked until midnight to plan amazing lessons for the following day, only to realize in the morning you were so tired that you could only shove the materials at your kids and have them work silently. (Also guilty — more times than I can count.)

When we take on too many obligations, we sacrifice the ability to feel like we're doing a good job on the things that matter. We look back on the previous months or years and think, *"How did I get here? Is the daily grind all there is? Is this really what my life has become?"*

> *The self-sabotage of overscheduling is how we get stuck in a low-level existence, spending our days on menial tasks and mundane errands that never move us toward our goals. We convince ourselves we don't have time to figure out a better way, and the best stuff in life passes us by because we can't prioritize it.*

The lesson from Carla's story is this: *You must leave room in your schedule for opportunity.* If someone offers you a chance to do something that will move you toward your goals, you want to have the time AND the mental bandwidth to say yes.

You can't let humdrum daily tasks consistently steal time away from what's most important. There has to be space in your life to break from the ordinary and do things that help you create the life you want to live.

You have to stop telling yourself "I never have time" and face the truth. If something is truly a priority, you'll MAKE time.

And if instead of making time, you find yourself making excuses for why it can't be done, know that in your heart, there's a part of you that doesn't really want to do it.

There's a fear or limiting belief that's keeping you from taking action. Maybe you're afraid it won't work out. Maybe you don't believe in yourself enough, or don't think the goal is possible for you.

Think about what's holding you back. If you really wanted it and believed you could do it, you'd make time for it. So why aren't you?

When you let go of limiting beliefs about who you are, how you can or should use your time, and what you could or should accomplish, then pursuing your ambitions won't feel silly or unattainable.

It will feel like an alignment between who you are and how you spend your time. You'll know what you want out of life, and feel empowered to shift your focus accordingly.

7

Aligning time with priorities to build a true legacy

Many people find themselves stuck in a never-ending daily grind because they don't know what they want their lives to look like or don't have big picture goals they're working toward. They're too busy to consider questions like:

- *How do I want to be spending my time?*
- *What do I want to accomplish in my life?*
- *What kind of legacy do I want to leave?*

Confusion or even a bit of low-grade panic is normal when you stop to think about what you actually want. Prioritizing your own desires may be a struggle for you, and feel selfish to even consider.

Maybe you weren't raised to think about different options for your life, or didn't have the privilege of making choices because so few were available. You might be used to survival mode only. Or maybe you once had an idea of what you wanted, but are now weighed down by supporting other people's dreams and have lost sight of your own vision.

Fortunately, none of these situations are a deal-breaker. You'll have a better sense of what you want and the goals you're working toward by the time you finish this chapter. At the very least, you'll know what you *don't* know, and will be attuned to uncovering the answers.

What do you want your legacy to be?

Think of your legacy as what you will leave behind when you're gone. Your legacy is the accumulation of your work, wisdom, and lived experiences, all of which have made a mark on the world.

Building a legacy may sound daunting, but the way you think about, define, and build a legacy will change throughout your lifetime. It's not a static concept you have to "get right" and "stick to."

I currently define the legacy I'm building in this way: helping other people live a more purposeful and conscious life by modeling that myself and sharing what I've learned with others. I want to show up in the world as the most healed, healthy, and whole person I can be, so that I can help others live that way, too.

Having at least a vague understanding of what you want your legacy to be is important for many reasons. But for the purposes of this book, a legacy is most useful as a tool to clarify your life choices and the way you spend your time.

It's likely that part of your legacy will include the impact you hope to make on some of your family members. You might see your primary legacy as the wisdom, heritage, and experiences you are able to gift to your children, nieces and nephews, or other young people who are like family to you.

Your legacy might also include adult family members, and supporting your partner, spouse, siblings, cousins, etc. in building their legacies. It could include caring for aging family members, and preserving and cherishing their legacies.

If any of these family-oriented connections are deeply important to you, choosing to see them as part of your legacy will change the way you use your time. Not only will you perceive time with these family members as more valuable than keeping a spotless house or whatever else is keeping you from them, the way you use your time when you're together will be different. You'll focus more on meaningful shared experiences.

Your legacy might also include the impact you make on the world through volunteer organizations, your religious community, or your talents and hobbies. When you choose to see these things as part of your legacy, they will no longer get your "leftover" time when all the mundane tasks are finished. These activities will get scheduled into your calendar first, because they are the things that enable you to feel like you're accomplishing your purpose on this planet.

Since you're a teacher, your legacy is also likely to include the impact you're making in the classroom. When you have a clear vision for your legacy as an educator — the mark you wish to have made on your students and the lasting impact on their development because of their time with you — it's amazing how clearly things come into focus.

Having a perfectly decorated classroom or mastering the latest tech tools may not feel quite so important. Showing up each day with presence, patience, and wisdom so you can be responsive to kids suddenly becomes the most critical work.

You stop obsessing over the annoyances of the job which pale in comparison, and spend most of your energy focusing on what you're really there to impart each day. How other people define your job and what they expect from you is no longer the driving force. The influence you want to leave behind on your students is your motivation to keep showing up.

This is the power of legacy. It shapes how you use your time, and impacts what you choose to focus on and give the majority of your attention to.

The free mini-course at FTBproject.com can help you think through your legacy in detail, but if you feel overwhelmed, don't overcomplicate this. When you take a few moments to be still with yourself, you'll probably be able to tap into your intuition and recognize the core of your legacy, even if you aren't sure of the specifics.

In other words, it's okay if you can't yet articulate exactly which values, wisdom, or traits you want to instill in your students or strengthen in your relationships. Just focus for now on the ways you want to make an impact on the world (through relationships, teaching, your art, volunteering, special skills, etc.). Get in touch with the things that could allow you to make your mark, in whatever way you can in your current season of life.

Keep in mind that living your legacy may not seem like anything grandiose. Maybe you love needlepoint, and it brings you joy to make something for others which they can display in their homes and pass down as family heirlooms. Needlepointing might be part of your legacy.

Maybe you love running, and you enjoy participating in local 5K races when you have time. Living your legacy can include running these races, as well as supporting and inspiring others to run (or live out dreams of their own).

Maybe you love encouraging other people each week at a community gathering, or bringing breakfast for your colleagues. These are simple ways that you leave your mark on the world, and they can be prioritized as part of your legacy.

When you have some understanding of your legacy, it becomes much easier to define your long-term goals, because you know what's most important to accomplish with your life.

Having your long-term goals will put you in a better position to develop short-term goals, and figure out what things you can be doing now to achieve the big picture things you want.

And having your short-term goals will help you decide how you want to structure your daily routines. You'll know which activities to give more time to and which to give less.

You won't just be muddling through day-by-day and giving your attention to whatever seems most urgent. You'll understand what's actually important so you can have the courage to do fewer things better.

How to build a legacy in your current season

Don't panic if you're thinking, "My life looks NOTHING like what I want, and I don't know how I'm supposed to build a legacy with all this chaos!"

Identifying your legacy is important, but it doesn't necessarily mean you have to focus on every aspect of it right now. If you're not currently building a legacy in one particular area, that doesn't mean it will never happen.

When we think of a life well-lived, we have to consider the various seasons of life, each of which may last weeks, months, or even years. These seasons of life are shaped by your circumstances.

If you have a family member in hospice care, you're in a season where you're focused on end-of-life issues and grieving.

If you have young children at home, you're in a season of pouring a tremendous amount of time and energy into being a caregiver.

Certain seasons of life require you to prioritize one aspect of life over another. When family or health issues are critical, building your legacy as a teacher will need to be a top priority in another season. You can engage in professional development at any time, but you cannot get back this season with your loved ones ever again.

It's critical to know which season of life you're in and plan your priorities accordingly.

Otherwise, you'll find yourself growing frustrated and overwhelmed by the pressure to accomplish goals that are more properly addressed in another season. It will take twice as much effort to do them now, and you'll get half the results.

In this way, fulfillment, purpose, and balance are not daily achievements. They are lifetime achievements.

You want to look back at your life many years from now and see that you spent seasons focusing on yourself, on your significant other, on your children, on making a home, on your career, etc., and that was exactly what you were supposed to have done at each point in time.

> *Think about what season of life you are in, and which priorities you SHOULD be focusing on in this season in order to further the next phase of your legacy.*
>
> *The goal is not to do everything you CAN each day but everything you SHOULD.*

Allow the way you build your legacy to change with different seasons of life, as well as with the seasons of the year.

You can probably look at your school and personal calendar, and tell which weeks or months are going to demand more of your time and energy.

There might be times when your partner, spouse, or co-parent has busy seasons at work, which means you have to pick up the slack. Or there might be certain times of year when you're spending far more time running around to various activities and social events.

Don't fight these natural patterns in the year — embrace them.

Life was not meant to be lived the same way every day. There is a time and season for everything.

You'll get nothing but frustration if you try to prioritize things during this season when something else is creating a time crunch.

Instead, spread out your priorities over time, knowing that both legacy and balance are about seeing things from the long-term.

As a teacher, you have some time off during the summer, and a number of three-day-weekends and week-long vacation periods throughout the school year. Those are times when you can choose to devote yourself to your family, friends, hobbies, and anything else you want or need to.

And just as tax accountants have an obvious busy season and know that their personal lives will be on hold from January through April, teachers also have times that are extra busy. The main one is the start of a new school year, but the end of year can also be extra demanding, as can report card and parent conference weeks.

It's okay for work to take center stage during those times. You shouldn't feel guilty about having busy seasons (as long as you're not making excuses and allowing *every* week to be your busy season where you neglect other priorities).

It's okay to work nonstop and barely spend any time at all on priorities apart from work during certain seasons, and it's okay for work to fall completely off your radar during other times of the year.

Figure out what works for your family and personality type, and remember that each season is different.

Identify the daily habits that contribute to your legacy

You begin creating your legacy when you show up as the best version of yourself each day — your true essential self — and engage in the kinds of activities that contribute to your desired legacy. The most important requirements are observation, reflection, mindfulness, and presence.

To put it more simply: Being frazzled 24/7 without a moment to think does not help you live out your true legacy. You can accomplish a lot of things by staying busy, but you'll miss out on the sense of fulfillment that comes from being truly intentional about your daily choices.

Because the biggest part of my legacy involves helping others live a purposeful, conscious life, I have to make sure my daily habits enable me to live that way myself.

Yoga, exercising, meditating, spending time in nature, taking mindfulness breaks, reading personal development books, listening to inspiring podcasts, etc. are not just fun hobbies for me. I can't hope to find "leftover" time for these things.

They are essential components of my life and core habits, because they enable me to build my legacy. If I were to do nothing but work, maintain a household, and try to squeeze in family time, I wouldn't have the physical, emotional, or spiritual bandwidth to leave the impact I want to on this world.

We're going to talk about self-care as a catalyst for productivity in the final section of the book, but for now as we focus on defining your legacy, think about the types of activities that enable you to be your best self.

If your legacy centers on your family, loved ones, friends, or life partner ... what kinds of things would you like to be doing on a regular basis to build that legacy? What activities would you like to engage in together? What types of conversations would you like to be having?

If your legacy centers on your work (either teaching or another pursuit you care deeply about), what aspects of that work feel most connected to your legacy and give you the greatest amount of fulfillment?

These are the things which should be your priorities in life. Again, you won't be able to do everything you want to right now, because the more mundane stuff has to be handled, too.

But there should be some elements of your regular life — not just things you do on a special occasion — that give you a deep sense of purpose and satisfaction. You can make some small shifts in your daily habits to build your legacy and move you toward long-term goals.

You don't have to give the most time to your biggest priorities

When I talk to teachers about the most important things in their lives, I usually hear one of two answers (and sometimes both). They mention some version of God/faith/spirituality, and family/loved ones.

Nearly all of these teachers feel guilty because they spend more time on things they say matter less, like watching TV and running errands. The guilt comes from an assumption that things which matter the most should get the most time.

But that's not necessarily true.

Your spirituality might be your top core value, but you'll always spend more time working and sleeping than you will praying, volunteering, or attending religious services.

Housework might be one of your lowest priorities, but you'll probably spend a lot more time cleaning and getting things done around the house than engaging in deeply fulfilling pursuits.

PRIORITIZATION AND LIVING YOUR LEGACY IS NOT ABOUT GIVING THE MOST TIME TO THE MOST IMPORTANT THINGS.

IT'S ABOUT MAKING SURE THAT THE MOST IMPORTANT THINGS DON'T CONTINUALLY GET SIDELINED BECAUSE OF LESSER PRIORITIES.

If your faith is really important to you, that doesn't mean you have to replace all your TV watching in the evenings with reading scripture. It means that you will look for daily rituals and small moments throughout your day to reconnect to your spirit. It means that you should set aside blocks of time on a regular basis for activities that allow you to experience something divine or sacred, and make sure nothing else consistently encroaches on that time.

You can insert any other life priority here: self-care, time with extended family, and so on. *Put that dedicated time for priorities in your calendar first*, and schedule everything else around it.

This sounds like a minor shift, but most people do the complete opposite. They try to do the lesser priorities first to "get them out of the way." They don't think they can relax until everything else is done.

But this means their top priorities only get the leftover time. And because it's so rare that every task is complete, very few people end up with any "leftover" time.

What if you gave yourself permission to enjoy your family BEFORE your papers were all graded in the evening? What if you set aside 15 minutes for self-care BEFORE doing laundry?

That way you could be sure these bigger priorities would actually take place, even if it was just for a short period of time, instead of hoping to have a bigger block of time for them when all the banal stuff is complete.

Imagine what your life would be like if you set aside even a few regular hours for exercising, hobbies, and people you care about, and then worked in all your unpaid schoolwork, errands, and housework around those things (instead of vice versa).

It's not about the amount of time. It's the consistency or regularity of the time that's important, and the refusal to let that time be disrupted by things which matter less.

5 steps to aligning daily life with your priorities

Let's look at some more concrete ways to implement these principles. I'm going to share a process we use in the 40 Hour Teacher Workweek Club to help members figure out what they want to spend their time on and allocate hours in their schedule accordingly.

I'll outline the process here in an explanatory style, but a more succinct, step-by-step system is available at FTBproject.com. You can download the free workbook there to help you complete this process and see additional examples from teachers who have done this.

Please take liberties and make this process your own. If you feel like going in a different order or structuring things differently, trust your intuition!

Step 1: Identify your non-flexibles

Think about the obligations that you cannot change, and things you have to do at specific times and days, and put them on the schedule.

Examples include:

- Contractual work hours
- Time spent commuting to work
- Recurring appointments, activities, and events for which you do not determine the time

Resist the urge to write in anything that's more flexible, like time for sleeping — we'll do that a bit later. This first step is about identifying anything that you feel strongly needs to be included and which must be done at predetermined times.

Get all of these non-flexibles penciled into your schedule (there probably won't be too many of them, as few things beyond work hours are totally out of our control). Color code them in red.

Step 2: List your top priorities that you want to uncover more time for

Think about the legacy you're trying to build. Consider the things you value most in life — the people and activities whom you want to prioritize, but don't know how.

List those out as categories. Many teachers will have 3-6 things listed, such as spouse/partner, kids/family, exercise, and hobby/self-care. Stay big picture, and think in broad categories so the list doesn't become overwhelming.

Step 3: Specify what life would look like if you prioritized these things

Now it's time to get more specific. Just about everyone wants more time for the people they care about, but what exactly does that mean for *you*?

Read over your priorities and envision what would your life would be like if you made appropriate time for them. Be specific, but don't overcomplicate this.

For example, prioritizing your partner might look like a weekly date night and no work after 8 p.m. Prioritizing kids might look like attending their tournaments on the weekends, and not working after 7 p.m. so you can spend time with them before they go to bed.

Just go with your gut instinct, and think about what would work for now, in this season of life.

Draw a big green square around these priorities.

Step 4: Add top priorities to the unallocated time in your schedule

See where you can add your top priorities to the open blocks of time in the calendar, and color code them in green.

You can pencil in open-ended categories, if you'd like. For example, put "Me Time" or "Self-Care" so you can define things how you want that day. Or, if you're not sure if you'll want to use a block of time to work on school stuff or just relax, put "Flex Time" so you can choose.

One teacher who uses this method simply pencils in "Priority Time." This is time in her schedule on a daily basis (some periods are longer than others) where she can choose to spend time on any of her core five priorities.

Step 5: Identify the in-betweens and add them to your schedule

Everything else in your life is in between a non-negotiable/inflexible task and a top priority which adds to your legacy. Put those things in the calendar when you'd ordinarily like to do them.

For instance, you might include:

- Sleep
- Meal prep/eating
- Housework
- Working on school stuff
- Errands

These are all things which matter and need to be done, but probably aren't what you want to design your life around. These items can fall into the spaces not occupied by your top priorities and non-flexibles.

Color code all of these items in yellow.

How to reduce time spent on low priorities to make time for higher ones

It's okay if you look at this schedule and feel like you don't have enough time for everything you care about.

It's also okay if this doesn't feel like a schedule you could keep every week.

You're only using this exercise to envision what life could be like if it was better aligned with your priorities. Every week won't be in perfect alignment. In fact, some weeks will be totally out of whack. That's normal and expected!

You can repeat this exercise quarterly to help you notice changes in the way you're using time, and to identify more areas where you can eliminate or streamline.

But it's not a schedule you will make yourself follow.

The goal is to understand where your time is going, and find ways to reduce the mundane tasks you've highlighted in yellow to make more time for the high priority items highlighted in green.

Go for the low-hanging fruit to begin with, and trust your instincts. Where do you have a hunch you are losing time, and could somehow cut out or reduce tasks?

Look at the schedule and mentally run through your day:

- Does it take you an hour to get out the door in the morning?
- Are you losing thirty minutes after school to chatting or checking social media?
- Is there an inefficient routine in your errands that sucks up your entire afternoon?
- Are you overcomplicating housework or doing it more often than needed?
- Is there a volunteer obligation you've outgrown or need to cut back on for now?
- Are you selecting assignments for students that create hours of grading for you every night?

Circle the blocks in your schedule that you might be able to streamline, reduce, or eliminate.

Then, pick three of those things to change immediately. You may want to choose the two easiest things which require little effort to reduce, and one thing that would make the biggest impact.

These three things will be your focus for the coming week (if you want to fast track success) or coming month (if you want a more manageable, sustainable approach). Fill that yellow time with green activities.

To make sure this exercise has a real impact on the way you use your time, here's the most important thing to remember:

 FLEXIBILITY IS IMPORTANT, BUT WHEN YOU MAKE TOO MANY EXCEPTIONS FOR YOUR PRIORITY TIME, THOSE THINGS WILL CEASE TO BE PRIORITIES IN YOUR LIFE.

One day, a sick family member keeps you from having time for a pre-scheduled priority. The next day, it's parent-teacher conferences. The day after that, you help a friend move. The day after that, you decide to grade papers instead.

And before you know it, the week is over, and you haven't dedicated any time at all to the things you really wanted to do.

While you won't be able to follow your ideal schedule each week, I encourage you to have at least one or two blocks of time for priorities which you refuse to give up for any reason beyond an emergency. If someone asks you to do something else, you can simply say, "I have another obligation during that time and I'm already committed to it."

Your commitments to yourself are just as important as the commitments you make to other people. Don't worry so much about letting others down that you let yourself down. Keep your commitment to the things that matter most to YOU.

"I don't know how to prioritize" really means "I'm not clear on what I want."

Maybe you're thinking at this point, *I know at least part of what I want my legacy to be, and I know the things that matter most.*

But how exactly do I begin freeing up time for priorities?

Here's something that might help you get more clarity.

When you find yourself saying, "I don't know how to cut back," that really means, "I'm not yet sure what my priorities are."

And when you tell yourself, "I don't know how to do fewer things," that really means, "I'm not clear on what I want less of."

Tony Robbins teaches that anytime you're feeling stuck on the HOW, you should keep working on the WHAT and WHY. Once you know what you want and why you want it, the how will become clear.

I've found that the more I practice being in tune with myself — my emotions, gut reactions, physical energy level, and the things that bring me joy and contentment — the easier it is to know intuitively what I want to do.

In other words, being clear on what you want becomes easier the more you observe, listen to, and trust yourself, and the "how" starts to feel obvious.

Begin by allowing yourself a period of stillness so you can tap into those feelings. This might require letting go of excuses that you're too busy to figure things out or too overwhelmed to do any big picture work. I promise this investment of time will pay off in dividends that are exponential.

Some people might find it easier to sit down and plan, but my mind tends to be clearer when I'm moving around or out in nature. Your time to think might be on a walk, sitting outside, or even relaxing in your bathtub. Just set aside a half an hour. It might be helpful to have a notepad nearby for jotting down insights, or your phone for recording a voice memo.

During this time to think, don't drive yourself crazy trying to figure out how to make your life the way you want it. Instead, allow a few minutes to think about your WHY. What's the reason you want to create change? Why do you want to do fewer things better? Try to be specific, as that will make it easier to figure out which things you need to take action on. Here's an example:

> ❝ *My WHY is to avoid missing out on things with my family. My kids need me right now and I feel sad when I think about all the important moments I wasn't present for. My motivation is to have more time with them and not be thinking about all the school work I "should" be doing when I'm hanging out with the family.* ❞

Next, think about WHAT you want. Visualize a clear outcome or result if you can. What would your life look like each day if you had more time for family? What things would you be doing with them that you're not doing now? What things *wouldn't* be part of your life if you were spending more time with family?

> ❝ *What I want specifically is to do something fun together on Saturday evenings instead of planning lessons. I also want to limit the days I bring work home so I'm not sending the kids to their room to play alone every afternoon. Of course, there's more I'd like to have, but those two main things would make a big difference.* ❞

I think you'll be surprised how quickly you are able to identity the WHY and the WHAT that are motivating you. It doesn't have to be a perfect articulation — just start with this initial point of clarity, and let things evolve naturally from there.

Now you're ready to figure out the HOW in our final step. How can you use your WHY to make the WHAT a reality? List all the possible ways for getting what you want, and steps you could take to get you where you want to be.

As you make a mental or written list, don't limit yourself to ideas that feel safe and easy. The real change comes from thinking creatively and having the courage to carve out a path for your life that you've never tried before:

If I want to have Saturday nights and a couple evenings a week to hang out with my family, I could stay later at school on Tuesday and Thursday when my kids are busy with after-school activities. I'd barely see them before bed, but I could be totally present the entire afternoon and evening on Monday, Wednesday, and Friday. That would let me have some days to focus entirely on work without feeling guilty about neglecting my kids, and some days to focus on my kids without neglecting work.

I could also set my alarm super early on Saturday mornings and lesson plan before my family wakes up. If that's not enough time, maybe the kids can play quietly for an hour or so in the morning, and I'll stop at 9 a.m. Whatever's not done, is not done — I can train myself to be more efficient and stop reinventing the wheel every week.

Oh, and maybe I could start giving my students two projects a month instead of three to reduce my planning and grading time. Those projects are what I'm usually stressing about on weekends, and assigning fewer of them would help.

And maybe I could use more of the assessments provided in the teacher's' guide instead of recreating my own every week, since that's often the task that makes me stay at school later.

Once you get thinking about WHAT you want and WHY, a lot of HOWS will begin to surface naturally.

You can get advice and suggestions from others, but filter their ideas through your own intuition to make sure the approaches will make sense for *you*. Deep down, you know what's right, if you can be still and present enough to connect to that wisest part of your spirit.

When you're done thinking through the ways you can create change, choose one of the ideas to implement. Begin experimenting. Notice what is working and do more of that. When you feel something is missing, iterate.

Never let yourself off the hook when "I don't know how" is limiting you, particularly in relation to freeing up time for what matters. Stop and get clear on what you want — your motivation for it, and the way you'd like things to be instead — and start brainstorming how you might get the results you want.

8

Making time for what matters and letting go of the rest

Once you know the things that matter most in your in life and what it would feel like to have more time for them, it's time to put strategies in place for streamlining.

In this chapter, you'll learn the mindset that helps you zero in on priorities and use your time more wisely. We'll focus on eliminating less important things, and if they must be handled, batching them so you don't feel perpetually bogged down in minutiae.

We'll also discuss when to choose productivity and when to just be present, along with ways to use small blocks of time with intention.

Plan, then execute — not both at the same time

Thinking in advance about what you want and how to get it will have far-reaching effects in your life. This is a habit that differentiates the truly productive, accomplished person from the person who stumbles through life "putting out fires" and attending to whatever seems most urgent in the moment.

If you don't enjoy planning, there will be a learning curve ahead. You'll need to practice writing things out *before* you take action rather than just jumping right in, and that will feel counter-intuitive.

But you won't be able to make time for everything that matters if you're always making decisions about your time in the moment.

Here's why.

Envision the end of the school day, when students have just been dismissed. You take a look around the room and think to yourself, *Okay, let's see, what do I need to do here to wrap up and get myself ready for tomorrow?*

The first thing you see is the board, which needs to be erased. You walk over to do that, and notice papers spilling out of the file holder next to the board, so you stop to tidy them up. Right then the phone rings, so you go back over to your desk to answer it, and glance down at your computer, where you can see a new email has popped up. When you finish the phone call, you respond to the email, and then glance at the clock.

Twenty minutes have passed. You wonder, *What was I doing again? Let's see ... oh right, erasing the board!* And you're back to square one.

If you frequently fall into this trap and find time slipping away, you might have assumed it's because you have a poor memory, or you're "getting old," or you just can't get a moment of undisturbed peace and quiet.

But you can solve this problem if you make the plan first, and then execute it.

Planning and execution are two separate brain functions, and you can't do both well at the same time. If you list out your priority tasks in advance, then when it's time to execute, all you have to do is take action.

Imagine how differently your afternoon would flow if the kids left and you looked down at a to-do list. On that list, you saw several well-defined tasks: prep four specific materials for tomorrow; answer emails in inbox; grade unit tests.

You wouldn't have to waste time wondering what you should do first, or trying to make sure you didn't forget anything. You wouldn't be wandering around the room attending to miscellaneous tasks that may or may not be a priority. You wouldn't keep stopping to do whatever catches your eye.

If you're exhausted, it's easy to get distracted because you don't have the mental bandwidth to figure out how to use your time. But if you've planned in advance (at the start of the week, or first thing that morning), all you have to do later is execute the plan you already figured out.

And THAT can be the difference between a low stress, productive afternoon and one in which you feel like you're spinning your wheels but going nowhere.

So, when you think of a task that needs to be done, don't allow yourself to launch into action mode right away. It's more efficient to think it out first, and write it down.

What exactly needs to be done? Do you have the time, energy, and resources right now to complete it, given everything else on your list? If not, when would be a better time?

Write it down on your to-do list, either for today or another day later in the week.

Allowing yourself to plan WHEN to complete the task will keep you from letting urgent things or new ideas steal time away from your larger priorities.

You'll have the big picture in mind and envision the complete scope of your tasks before you begin. You won't have to redo tasks later because you didn't fully think them out before you started. Taking that minute to plan first can save you hours of time when you're ready to execute.

Even if you decide to complete the task right away, I still recommend writing it down. The likelihood of an unexpected interruption is pretty high, and you might lose your train of thought midway through. And if you're not interrupted, it's still a great feeling to be able to cross something off your list right away.

Prioritize tasks with a list-making system

Having a place to write down these tasks as they come to mind is critical. In fact, getting yourself in the habit of making prioritized to-do lists is a simple way to solve a lot of pervasive problems:

- No more keeping a running list of big projects and small tasks in your head.
- No more lying in bed at night thinking about all the things that didn't get done.
- No more 75 item to-do lists that make you want to quit before you even start.
- No more wasted time trying to figure out what to do first and what's really important.

Even if you've never been successful with a list-making system in the past, I encourage you to keep experimenting.

It's imperative that you find a way to get information out of your head and onto a list. If you don't write something down, it will take up space in your mind which could otherwise be used for creative problem-solving and being productive. Holding information in your mind is also very stressful. You'll feel like you can never stop thinking about work if you're always trying to remember everything you need to do.

So, when you're driving or resting or grocery shopping and suddenly think of a task, write it down, and then dismiss the thought from your mind.

You can use any list-making system or tool you'd like. Paper or digital lists are fine, and some people like a combination of the two.

The secret to a good list-making system is that it must force you to prioritize. The one I created for my classroom practice is now a fundamental part of the 40 Hour Teacher Workweek Club, and has been used by tens of thousands of teachers. I promise you — this approach is a game changer!

I designed the system as a weekly to-do list. That way, you have all seven days in front of you at once. Each weekday's list is broken into four sections: before school, during your lunch/prep period/break, after school, and at home.

There are only about five task slots for each time period. This balances the natural human tendency to underestimate how long things will take. We tend to plan our time according to a best-case scenario, and fool ourselves into thinking that if everything goes just right, we'll be able to fit more in.

By only allowing yourself to plan a handful of tasks during each portion of the day, you won't set yourself up for failure with an unrealistic list. Each time you think of something new that needs to be done, you can't just add it to a long list of things which you're somehow expected to tackle all at once.

You're making a decision right away about the optimal, realistic time period for completing the task, and adding it to that slot.

If a task crops up mid-morning and you notice your afternoon slots are already full, you'll realize you either need to schedule the new task for the next day in an open slot, or move something you'd planned for today to the following day. With a limited number of task slots, you won't be trying to squeeze an impossible or overwhelming amount of work into a single time period.

There's obviously a bit more to the process and it sometimes takes experimentation to tweak the system to fit your personality. But for our general purpose here in this book, the most important thing is to practice these four habits:

- **Marking important, inflexible events on a calendar:** This ensures you won't forget anything important, helps you avoid overscheduling because you can see at a glance which days are busy, and helps you batch similar tasks so you're more efficient (i.e. if you have an appointment across town on the 25th, you can schedule other errands for that same day).

- **Getting EVERYTHING out of your head and onto a list:** When you think of something that needs to be done, write it down somewhere, and then each evening or morning as you're planning out the day, schedule those tasks into a slot on your weekly to-do list (or put it on a long-term priorities list so you can schedule it in for a future week.)

- **Consulting your list before you start working instead of just tackling random things as they pop into your head:** Since you've decided in advance which tasks are most important for the day and you know what you want to accomplish before school, during your prep, and after school, all you have to do is execute during those times.

- **Emptying the day's to-do list and placing any incomplete tasks elsewhere:** It will probably be rare that you're able to cross everything off your list because of last-minute interruptions and tasks taking longer than planned. Give yourself the sense of satisfaction that comes from having an empty to-do list, anyway, and move everything that's incomplete to another day (or to a long-term priority list if the task wasn't urgent after all). Then you can rest easy, knowing you've allotted time to the task and it will get done soon. While you're doing this, look at the other days' lists and see if there's anything you can eliminate or push back so you're focused on the biggest priorities rather than trying to do everything.

Use the 4-question test to help you eliminate tasks

Even with a good list-making system, it's common to struggle with prioritization. How do you figure out which items will get done today and which ones won't? What happens when you don't have enough time for everything that feels urgent and important?

Let's say this is your to-do list for after school:

- ☐ Finish and submit report cards
- ☐ Finalize tomorrow's lessons
- ☐ Grade quiz kids took today
- ☐ Return parent phone call
- ☐ Contact museum to ask about field trip

This might be too much to do in a single afternoon, unless you're planning to stay quite late. The most important thing is probably submitting your report cards, assuming they're due within the next day or so. That means you should prioritize (make time for) that task first.

Finish your report cards, and then think about your remaining time and capacity to focus. If you won't be able to do the rest of the tasks, give them the prioritization test.

Ask yourself:

- *Does it really need to be done?*
- *Does it really need to be done by me?*
- *Does it really need to be done by me right now?*
- *Does it really need to be done to the full extent by me right now?*

If the answer is no to every question, it's probably not a priority, and you can try to eliminate it from your schedule for today. Put it on your to-do list for another day, or on a long-term priorities list that you'll revisit in a few weeks.

You might find that calling the parent doesn't really need to be done — the parent asked a question which can be answered in an email which you can dash off quickly. Though a phone call would be preferable, an email will need to do, since you've got so many other things on your plate.

Contacting the museum might not need to be done by you if your whole team is going on the field trip — make a note to ask your team leader the next day at lunch for the info you need.

Grading the kids' quiz might not need to be done today — if it takes two days to get the assignment back instead of one, that's still acceptable. Or, you might decide it doesn't need to be done by you, and you can have the kids self-assess the following day as part of your re-teaching.

Finalizing tomorrow's lesson might not actually need to be done at all (stick with the original plan and don't create more work by redoing it with alternative ideas at the last minute) or it might not need to be done today (you may want to wait until morning to make final decisions).

You have to get real with yourself: There are not enough hours in the day to do everything you'd like, to the full extent you'd like to do them. You'll need to take a shortcut somewhere, or delay something, or eliminate something altogether.

This is not being lazy. This is what the most productive, accomplished people do all day long. They weigh out their obligations to determine where their time and energy is best spent, and they're realistic about how much they can actually get done.

Productive people know that their work to-do list can become never-ending if they're not intentional about keeping it in check, and there are too many other priorities to allow that.

So, when you're feeling overwhelmed by the thought of all the things which need to be done by you right now, ask yourself some prioritization questions. It often becomes clear that you have some flexibility, and can intentionally delay, eliminate, or simplify a few things in order to create time for the things which absolutely must be done.

Once you've removed the stress of "I have to do everything right now" by considering other possibilities, you can then go back to the list and re-evaluate through a new lens:

66 *Which of these are the best things for me to focus on right now? None of it is life-or-death. To make it easier on myself later in the week, I could tackle a couple of things now. Maybe I'll go ahead and look over my lesson plans, and I could call the parent back on my drive home. That will make me feel like I got some important things done and takes some of the pressure off me tomorrow.* 99

Whatever doesn't actually get done that day should get moved to another day's to-do list, and scheduled into a specific time slot (i.e. before school on Tuesday or planning time on Wednesday). That way, you can feel a sense of closure for now, and make sure you begin tomorrow with a realistic list rather than playing an impossible game of catch up.

There will certainly be days when tons of things really do have to be done to the full extent by you right away. However, learning to prioritize tasks will keep your stress levels down, and prevent you from feeling constantly overwhelmed by the pressure to do everything all at once. It's an essential practice for doing fewer things better.

Create a buffer day for life's little annoyances

Often it's the "little things that kill you" when it comes to feeling on top of your tasks. Many of our to-do lists are cluttered with small stuff that steals our time and energy away from the bigger and more meaningful tasks:

- ○ Call cable company about incorrect billing
- ○ Fix broken shelf
- ○ Take package to post office
- ○ Organize digital resources for upcoming unit
- ○ Empty email inbox
- ○ Clean out freezer

There's nothing less motivating for me than waking up in the morning to see a to-do list filled with those tasks on top of all the more important things I need to get done. How can I find time to concentrate on a bigger project (like writing this book!) when there's all these small tasks that also need to be done?

I can't do both well at the same time. And so I don't try.

Instead, I put these minor tasks on my to-do list for Sundays, so that I can use the rest of the week to focus on what's really important to me. I focus on the big stuff — the projects that move me toward my goals — five or six days a week, and I use Sunday as my "buffer day" to handle life's little annoyances.

I give myself permission to write those distracting tasks down on my buffer day's to-do list, and then I can forget about them until Sunday. They're no longer hanging over my head, because I'm not "supposed to" be doing them right away.

Then when my buffer day arrives, I don't attempt to do any big projects or work. I just knock out all the little things that accumulated throughout the week.

Sometimes that takes an hour and I have the rest of the day on Sunday to relax; sometimes my buffer tasks require the whole afternoon. But either way, batching them gives me a real sense of satisfaction. I'm able to whip through a lot of nagging details in one very productive day. And, I'm not thinking about all the more important things I wish I could be doing. It's my buffer day, and the little things are all I need to do.

If I see the buffer day to-do list is growing too long or some of the tasks can't wait until Sunday, sometimes I'll do half a buffer day on Wednesday. That means I set aside part of the day to stop doing my regular work and catch up on the little things.

You might want to have one buffer day for your home and personal life, and one buffer day for catching up on school-related things.

> *The idea is to do these kinds of tasks all at once, so you don't spend every day swamped with de-energizing minutiae. This also allows you to have substantial blocks of time throughout the rest of the week to get more important things done.*

For example, moving those annoying tasks to a buffer day might free up more time on Mondays for you to get all your lesson planning done. Monday can now be your lesson planning day. Tuesdays and Thursdays could be your grading days, Wednesdays could be your errand and appointment days, and so on.

On Wednesdays, you won't have to freak out because the stack of papers to grade keeps growing. You know you have Thursday set aside for that. And on Friday, you won't have to worry about all those emails that went unanswered — you have your buffer day on Sunday when you'll be able to catch up.

You're batching similar tasks and creating "theme days" so you can do the most important tasks without feeling distracted by everything else. This doesn't mean you can only grade or plan on certain days, but having designated time set aside will keep you from feeling like you need to be doing everything on your to-do list at once.

Decide how to eliminate the tasks you repeatedly put off

I am always looking for ways that I create extra work for myself or set unnecessary goals that I should stop pressuring myself to achieve. Because we all have far more things we'd like to do than we actually have time for, the ideal response to having too many tasks is to get rid of them altogether.

Deciding that you're not going to do something isn't a failure. It's a goal.

Notice when you're putting off tasks over and over again with no real consequence: *reorganize the filing cabinet; clean out old gardening supplies; explore resources on sixteen new websites from that training last month,* and so on.

If these things weren't important enough to get done week after week, why were they even on your list of things to do? They just aren't a big enough priority compared to everything else in your life.

Rather than pretend tomorrow will be different and keep assigning the tasks to yourself over and over again, face the truth: They don't really need to be done by you right now, and probably won't be super important anytime in the foreseeable future. Some things shouldn't be on the to-do list at all.

Other tasks can be partially eliminated: They *will* need to be done, but not right away. Or, they could be done to a lesser extent or with less frequency, or handed off to someone else. All of these approaches will help you eliminate at least a portion of the work so it's not so time-consuming.

Let's think through a task that most of us hate: putting away laundry. If you've written "fold clothes" on your list but have too many other things that are more important, cross off the clothes folding from today's list and write it down for tomorrow. Then, evaluate it again. Does it feel like a priority for that day, compared to everything else you've written down? If so, it should come before other tasks that aren't urgent. If not, try scheduling it for the next day.

When you start to notice the same thing not passing the prioritization test over and over, that's a sign you shouldn't be putting it on your to-do list daily, because it's clearly not that important. You can permanently make clothes folding into a buffer day task, and stop pressuring yourself to handle it at any other time.

This may require an examination of your personal standards. You might expect yourself to have all laundry folded perfectly and put away as soon as it's been washed, but that's probably just a preference, habit, or norm you were raised with. It's not indicative that clothes folding is the best and highest use of your time.

Maybe you need to relax your standards a bit, and try a different approach to free up time for something that ultimately matters more. What if you got rid of all the things you never wear so you don't have to fold everything into tiny rolls to make it all fit? You could invest time in cleaning out your dresser, and then reap the benefits daily of being able to find what you need at a glance without everything needing to be packed in perfectly tight.

You might also want your family members to step up and take responsibility. My friend Diane has three daughters who started taking their clothes out of the dryer and putting them in drawers when they were 3 years old. (Sorting is a preschool skill, after all: find the dresses, put them in the top drawer; find the pants and put them in the middle drawer, etc.). It was a fun activity when they were little, and now that they're older, it's never crossed their minds that a parent would put away their laundry for them.

Don't be afraid to experiment. If you or your family members don't have immaculately organized dresser drawers and yet the earth's still spinning on its axis, you might decide it feels pretty good not to spend all your weekends folding laundry the "right" way.

> *Remind yourself that finding easier ways to complete tasks is not a moral shortcoming or a failure to handle basic adulting. Let go of labels, judgments, and assumptions about the tasks on your to-do list, and figure out whether you can release some of the expectations you've created.*

No one knows or cares what's inside your dresser drawers except you. When you realize you're making extra work for yourself, that's a victory in the battle for more free time. You're releasing that self-imposed pressure to focus on things that don't matter much.

I think you'll find there's a lot of things on your to-do list that fall under this category … if you're willing to question your habits and be honest with yourself about what actually needs to be done, and what would just be *nice* to have done.

You might notice that "change bulletin board" has been pushed back on your list three or four times, which is a sign that it's not a priority. Instead of expecting yourself to change your boards monthly, try quarterly. Or at the very least, make sure you pick a theme that's not seasonal so you can leave the displays up longer and the task won't need to be prioritized again so soon. You might even be able to leave the same background and border up all year, and have students be responsible for rotating out their best work.

As another example, you might discover that "find culminating project ideas" for an upcoming unit of study never seems to pass the prioritization test. You might realize you already planned most of your unit and it's pretty solid without a new final project idea. Remove that task from your list.

You have enough pressure to Do All The Things, and it's incredibly freeing to get real with yourself about what's never going to happen.

Let the unnecessary reveal itself through what is continually left undone. Then prioritize the important tasks you've been procrastinating on, and find ways to eliminate all or part of your lesser priorities.

Use small blocks of time with intentionality

I hope you can see that "fewer things better" is not synonymous with "get more things done faster."

It's about identifying where your time is best spent and minimizing the rest of your tasks so they don't feel like a constant distraction. That's a process which requires intentionality.

Intentionality will mean that being productive is your focus for some parts of the day. Those are the times when you want to achieve goals and get things done.

Other times, intentionality will mean recognizing that you need a moment of stillness, or to be present in the experience. Maybe you're having a teachable moment with your class, or your pet wants to snuggle with you while you're trying to clean up.

Letting go of the plan and being present in the moment is also part of doing fewer things better. It's recognizing that the unexpected is a bigger priority, and what you thought you needed to do can be handled later.

Practice tuning in to what's most needed in any given moment for you to stay balanced. Notice how it feels when you push yourself to keep working, and how it feels to stop and be present, and learn from those experiences.

I find that if I force myself to keep being productive when the last rays of the sunset are streaming through the window, the extra three minutes of accomplishment doesn't bring me half the satisfaction of taking a break. Walking over to the window and gazing out to admire the light rejuvenates me. So, I let myself stop and enjoy that whenever possible.

The opposite is true when I linger in bed too long in the morning. Those few extra minutes of feeling the warm covers draped over my shoulders aren't really worth it. I'll feel much better if I get moving, because then I won't have to rush so much. Those are times when I try to gear myself into productivity mode as quickly as possible.

I encourage you to be intentional about when to be productive and when to be present.

Take advantage of every moment so that you are either getting things done, or allowing yourself to have a time of pleasure and enjoyment. Shift things around constantly on your to-do list so that you can prioritize what is truly important in that moment and be flexible as new things come up.

If you're spending most of your time either getting things done or savoring the moment, you'll generally feel good about how you spent your day. It's the pacing around or sitting in agitation while waiting that feels bad. It's the letting time slip away on mindless activities that you'll wish you hadn't done.

 THE ONLY TIME THAT'S WASTED IS THE TIME THAT YOU NEITHER UTILIZE NOR ENJOY. EVERY EXPERIENCE IS AN OPPORTUNITY FOR FULFILLMENT THROUGH GETTING THINGS DONE OR BEING MINDFULLY PRESENT.

Even a boring meeting which feels like a waste can be productive if you focus on what it's accomplishing for you, or if you choose to enjoy the chance to sit and relax passively for awhile. You can make the time meaningful and satisfying depending on what you choose to focus your attention on.

What's awesome about this mindset is that small amounts of time can have the biggest impact. You never have to write off a block of time because you think it's too short to get things done, and just fritter it away on things you don't actually want or need to do.

I find that when I only have 15 minutes, I often get more done than if I have 45 minutes, because I stop procrastinating and overthinking. I know I can't afford to waste time, and I work with more focus.

So when you find yourself with only six minutes until your lunch break is over, don't just check your phone. Ask yourself,

What do I need right now? Is there a small task on my to-do list that would feel really good to take care of? Or do I need a moment to catch my breath and center myself? What's the best use of this time for me?

Making the most of every moment doesn't necessarily mean getting things done every moment. Listen to your body. Pay attention to the signals of when to rest and when to work. The more you can go with the flow instead of forcing yourself to act in a way that's counter to your feelings, the more naturally productive you will become.

9

Eliminating the unnecessary from class time

Now that you've clarified what's most important in your personal life and understand how to allocate your time accordingly, let's apply these principles to your time with students. What does it look like to allocate instructional time to what's most important?

Well, I'll tell you what it *doesn't* look like.

At the end of our animal adaptations unit one spring, I designed a project for my third graders that I knew would be the perfect culminating activity. The task involved designing an original animal which had specific characteristics for surviving in its habitat. Students had to research, write, and present about it, as well as create a physical model of their animal.

When I designed the project, I ensured it checked all the innovative teaching boxes: student choice, technology integration, higher level thinking, student self-evaluation, and so on.

What I neglected to do, however, was *carve out enough time in our schedule for students to complete it.*

I made time for the more academic portion, but the designing a model part was taking a LONG time, and it was making a gigantic mess in the classroom. I dedicated two class periods to it and figured anyone who wasn't done could just work on it for bell work.

To be honest, I didn't have a plan. And when over 60% of the class wasn't anywhere near finished at the end of the second class period, I didn't know what to do.

My brilliant idea was to procrastinate on trying to figure out a solution, and just keep putting it off. I basically forgot about the project and hoped the kids would, too.

The problem is, they didn't forget. This was one of the most engaging activities they'd done all year, and they were very attached to their animals. Every day, the kids were asking me, "When do we get to work on our animals some more? When can we take them home?"

I just kept putting them off. "Well, if we can finish XYZ, we're going to do it Friday afternoon … " And of course, Friday would come and we'd always run out of time.

Eventually most of the class stopped asking, but there was that *one kid* who would have persisted all the way up through the last day of school: "How come we never finished making our animals?"

So I finally just tossed out a lesson I was planning to teach one day and gave the class a much longer period of time than I could afford to allocate to this, and then whatever wasn't done they had to finish at home, which means it never really happened.

Cue the *wah wah wah wah* trumpet, right?

It's a terrible feeling to know that you got your students excited about starting something that you'll never give them enough time to finish.

It's such a letdown to introduce a great idea, and then just let it fizzle out because you didn't prioritize it in your schedule.

You see, I knew when I designed this activity that it was going to be powerful. It was going to be a much better use of students' time than watching another video about animal adaptations, or filling in a worksheet on it, or giving them a quiz about it.

And yet, *I didn't prioritize the project.*

It was too much trouble to decide what I should cut out, and all my colleagues were doing the complete set of workbook pages. So, I just left the regular activities in the unit and tried to do too much.

> *The unfortunate truth is that most teachers are doing the exact same thing: dedicating hours to creating lessons they're not going to have time to implement.*

If you never have enough time to get through everything in your plans — if you're always days or weeks behind — you're probably over-planning.

And that means you're creating unnecessary work and frustration.

Plan your lessons for a realistic (rather than ideal) day

I planned my animal adaptations unit the way most teachers plan: according to an ideal day.

If things go well and there's no interruptions, we SHOULD have time to get through all of this.

But when was the last time you had an ideal day? When was the last time you got through an entire class period without an interruption or something unplanned derailing your lesson?

ALL THOSE UNEXPECTED INTERRUPTIONS AREN'T ACTUALLY UNEXPECTED. THEY HAPPEN EVERY SINGLE DAY. AND THAT MEANS YOU CAN PLAN FOR THEM.

You don't have to schedule yourself down to the minute. Instead you can allow some margin.

Think about a piece of notebook paper. The margins are there to keep you from writing all the way to the edge and running out of room for things that need to be added later. Also, it's less taxing to read a paper in which margins have been observed, because there's some white space. It's easier to find the most important ideas because the entire page isn't cluttered with content.

Similarly, you need margin in your instructional day, and margin in your life. Have some of that white space around the edges. Don't pack in so much.

Creating margin can be done by adding buffer time to your schedule. That doesn't mean having blank spots in your lesson plans where kids are sitting idly. It means you're more generous in your estimates of how long things will take so you don't have to rush.

Building in buffer time might mean turning part of a unit into a lesson, or a lesson into a ten minute read-aloud or video to expose students to the concept. It might mean eliminating the second half of a project, or cutting out a review activity.

These choices allow you to keep only the most impactful activities and go deeper with them. You'll have time for students' questions, addressing misconceptions, meaningful discussions, and teachable moments.

Any interruptions that occur won't stress you out, because the buffer time you've allowed means you won't be thrown hopelessly off schedule.

> *The idea is not to skip topics, skills, or standards altogether, but to be more realistic in the amount of <u>experiences</u> you plan for each one.*

This does require making hard choices. But when we refuse to do that, we find ourselves perpetually rushed and overscheduled.

And when we're overscheduled, sticking to The Plan becomes more important than engaging with the kids.

We get more attached to what's written down than to what's happening right in front of us. We can't eliminate anything from The Plan because we spent the entire weekend writing it and everything is equally important and it all HAS to get done.

We find ourselves caught in the trap of trying to keep as many things in the curriculum as possible, and we don't even realize it's happening. Literally nothing can be eliminated:

- *I have to keep that lesson because the kids really like it.*
- *I have to keep that one because my principal really likes it.*
- *I have to keep that one, because all my coworkers do it and it will look bad if I don't participate.*
- *I have to keep that one because I've done it every single year since I was student teaching and I'm sentimental about it.*
- *I have to keep that one because I paid to download it online and don't want to waste my money.*
- *I have to keep that one because I spent all weekend designing it from scratch by myself and there's no way I'm letting that hard work go to waste.*

Of course, these thoughts aren't happening on a conscious level.

We don't have the time or energy to think about WHY we insist on including all of these elements in our lesson plans. We just do it.

And then our students come in the door and we say, "Okay, everyone, let's get started, we have a lot to do today. I'm not answering that now, because we have ten more questions we need to go over in the next three minutes. No, I can't explain that again because we need to finish this. Let's go, let's go, let's go! We're running out of time!"

We rush through our day, and we rush our students through their day.

We feel this constant burden to fit more in and cram every single moment with a meaningful learning opportunity, and we push that burden on to students so that everyone feels anxious.

But there's no amount of rearranging your schedule which will magically allow time for every activity you want to include.

When you're sick of feeling like you never have enough time to teach everything you need to, the only choice is to do fewer things better.

Streamline elements of the school day that waste time

It's surprisingly easy to let class time slip away, especially when you have the same group of kids all day long. In many elementary schools, for example, it's common for time to be spent this way:

- 5 minutes to take attendance and lunch count
- 15 minutes to collect homework and have kids copy new assignments
- 15 minutes for bathroom breaks
- 5 minutes for lining up before lunch
- 10 minutes to get drinks after recess

- 20 minutes at dismissal for passing back papers, putting on coats, stacking chairs, etc.

We don't even realize how much time we're losing to these aspects of the day, because it's *just how we do school.*

Do these tasks provide so much educational value that they're worthy of consuming over an hour of your day? An hour a day is probably close to a quarter of the instructional time where students are in your room. No wonder you feel like you never have enough time for what really matters!

Every teacher — at every grade level — has elements of the school day which are less valuable than others. Some routines are truly unnecessary and can be eliminated altogether, while others are unavoidable but can still be streamlined to some extent.

Think through some ways you might restructure elements of your school day to get a better return on the investment of time. Here are some examples to get you thinking.

Bell work or morning work: Is the assignment students do when they first enter your classroom just something to keep them busy and quiet while everyone's settling in, or is it truly meaningful? Think about what's the best and highest use of their time when they're in your classroom. Is there something you value but can't often squeeze in (like reading, research, collaboration, centers, or projects) that kids could do as bell work instead?

Homework: There's a large body of research fully supporting *no* homework at the elementary level and showing that most secondary students are being assigned far more than is truly valuable. If you do need to give homework, do you have to assign it every night? My district required me to use the same homework assignments as my team, but I decided to only collect and assign homework on Fridays. This increased completion rates, since students had seven full days to do the work (Friday to Friday), and I only had to spend class time managing homework one day a week.

Student planners/reading logs: Many elementary teachers lose 5-10 minutes a day on checking student planners. This is solely an accountability measure (to ensure parents have signed off on things, kids have written down the book titles they read, etc.). Ask yourself — is this the best use of our time? Could students pair up and discuss the books they read the night before instead? Could a student helper (perhaps one person at each team) be in charge of making sure important notes have been copied correctly? Is there another way to convey info to parents that's more efficient?

Transition times: If you wait until your class "settles down" to begin instruction, you're going to lose tremendous amounts of instructional time. Use timers and countdowns, and when time is up, get started just like you said you'd do, letting stragglers catch up without acknowledging them except to help as needed. If you're consistent with this, students will learn you mean what you say and they have to keep pace. Try getting students focused immediately with a specific task that's an "easy win." For example, if you want groups of students to prepare for a lab, ask them to assemble the materials they need and hold up a specific item when they've found it. If you want students to open a book in preparation for discussion, say, "Please turn to page 214 and find the word *quintessential*. Put your finger on that word and be prepared to talk about what it means in the context of the paragraph. Ready? Page 214. I'll know you're ready when I see your finger on the word *quintessential*." These kinds of practices will get kids focused immediately on your instruction, instead of getting materials out and chatting while they wait for everyone else. Look for ways to make the transition task part of the lesson rather than downtime.

Dismissal: Try doing your most engaging activities at the end of the class period so students aren't watching the clock as much. Set the tone by structuring the day with focused work that continues until the very end of class, rather than using the last ten minutes on a "catch all" time for kids' miscellaneous tasks, cleaning up, asking questions about homework, etc. I dislike ending the day on a chaotic note, so I had my third graders work until 1:57 p.m. for a 2:00 p.m. dismissal. On my signal, they had 30 seconds to clean up and put things away, and then the first team ready was called to grab their backpacks and come sit on the carpet at the front of the room to chat quietly. The whole class could be cleaned up and have coats/backpacks on in three minutes, because that's all they needed to do, and they were motivated to leave on time. None of the chair stacking or room shutdown procedures happened until after most of the class had been dismissed, and the handful of late leavers took care of it.

These are simply ideas to get you questioning the way we've traditionally "done school."

But don't settle for ineffective procedures until someone gives you a suggestion that's a perfect fit for your teaching context.

It's the process of self-reflection and experimentation that enables you to determine what "fewer things better" will look like in your classroom. Think about the elements of your day which could be streamlined, and then examine the instruction itself.

Eliminate good learning activities to make time for the best

Many teachers find themselves consumed with finding and preparing activities for kids. We're over-planning stuff for them to do, when what they really need is authentic experiences with the skills.

For example, we all know from both research and common sense that students become better readers when they have more time to actually read. Kids need time to lose themselves in a book and practice reading for a sustained period of time.

And yet, most of our reading and English Language Arts instruction is spent having students *do activities about reading.* Kids spend most of their class time answering comprehension questions, summarizing, analyzing sentences, and so on, often in a format that prepares them for The Test.

We are spending endless unpaid hours creating and curating activities and tests and worksheets and quizzes, then tracking it all and reminding students to turn it all in.

And we never have time to ask ourselves: *Is the impact on student learning proportionate to the class time expenditure? Is this activity or strategy worth giving up all this time? Is there something else kids could be doing that is more impactful?*

I want you to be brutally honest in your self-reflection here. Unless your district requires you to follow a literal script and you must read every word of every lesson line-by-line, then you have *some* level of autonomy in your instruction, and you owe it to yourself and your students to exercise that autonomy.

Don't deflect and insist you "have no choice" but to teach the way you do. Consider the elements of your instruction where you do have some choice in deciding the best way to implement an activity or move kids toward learning outcomes.

Ask yourself: *How can I eliminate the good to make time for the great?*

Here are some ideas to get you thinking. Try not to judge these suggestions through a right/wrong or always/never dichotomy. I'm simply asking you to consider whether they are the best and highest use of your time:

Watching videos: Videos are a powerful way to communicate ideas. But is every video you're using the best way to help kids learn, or is it simply the easiest way? Are you showing all the videos by default because they're part of your curriculum, or choosing only the ones which are most beneficial for your students? Is watching the entire segment the best use of class time, or might it be more effective to play part of it and use the rest of your time for discussion? Would it be helpful to flip your homework by having kids watch the video on their own time and use class time for collaborative work?

Student presentations: Many teachers have kids conduct projects and then present their learning. However, two or three dozen student presentations consume a massive amount of class time, and kids tend to tune out after listening to the first few. What if students presented to groups of 4-5 people instead of to the whole class? They'd still get all the benefits of presenting and learning from peers, but in a much more condensed period of time.

Coloring, illustrating, and chart making: Unless you teach very young students who need the fine motor practice, think about how these activities might be stealing away time from work that is more impactful. Some kids will spend five minutes making a line in their chart perfectly straight and endlessly color-code their notes. You could give students explicit permission to turn in illustrations that aren't "perfect" and emphasize that they are not being graded on their drawing abilities. Model how to draw illustrations quickly, demonstrating how it's not necessary to spend more than 30 seconds making a diagram. Teach elementary kids how to illustrate a math problem by drawing quick circles instead of the actual objects in a word problem.

Activities where only one student is actively learning at a time: I remember a game my teachers used to play called "Around the World." At any given time, only one student was actively learning (being asked to solve a problem), and if you got your problem wrong, you were "out" and didn't participate for the rest of the activity. The kids who needed the most practice got the least of it. Of course, we still cheered anytime we got to play the game — it was easier and more fun than doing worksheets. But we weren't excited because we were actually learning, and student enthusiasm is not an effective measure of which activities are worthwhile. What if the teacher had every student follow along and solve each problem at their seats, and turned it into a team competition instead? Any activity in which only part of your class is engaged is worth questioning. Pay attention to times when the majority of the class is waiting passively (perhaps while one student solves a problem at the board) and consider how to make that time more valuable for everyone.

Required (but boring/ineffective) test prep and worksheets: Be creative, and look for ways to make required activities more valuable for students. If you must give a specific worksheet that isn't the best use of class time, make it more engaging by cutting the problems apart and having students play a game of Scoot so they're actively moving around the room. (Directions can be found with a quick internet search.) Or, minimize the time allocated to the worksheet by not making the kids wait for the whole class to finish and then reviewing the answers together. Instead, set up a grading station with copies of the answer key and ink pens. Students can get immediate feedback by self-assessing at the grading station, and if they show you they've mastered the skill, they can move on immediately to an activity that's a better use of their time.

Having kids answer an entire page of questions: Chances are good that you can tell after a handful of problems whether a student "gets it." Does it make sense to use up more class time and wear students out by assigning the whole page? I'd sometimes allow kids to stop after ten problems and show them to me; if they got them all right, they'd be allowed to work on something else. This motivated students to pay attention to accuracy rather than just rushing to complete the page. If they didn't get all ten right, I'd address the misconception and have them try five more. You can also have students do just the even or odd numbers on a page, or choose any 15 problems on the page they'd like. This tiny bit of control has a surprising effect on student motivation, takes up less class time, and creates less grading for the teacher. Just because the entire page of problems is there doesn't mean it's the best use of time to have students complete it.

As you consider these ideas, recognize that *you* are the primary expert on your students and teaching context.

Only you understand the full scope of what's needed and required in your instruction.

So only you can ask yourself, *Are the activities I'm spending so much time planning worthy of the instructional time devoted to them?*

Kids don't necessarily learn more because a research project requires seven sources instead of four. They don't become more knowledgeable about a subject area by spending an hour rearranging text on a slide. And once they've proven they know how to do something, they don't necessarily need to keep doing it over and over.

If you can find just a couple of things in your instruction to streamline or eliminate, that might free up an extra hour or two a week for more impactful activities.

"Kill your darlings" when everything doesn't fit

Identifying the elements of your instructional day to eliminate or streamline is an important first step. The next step is to gather the courage to let go of these familiar ways of teaching, which we're often rather attached to.

An unlikely person we can learn from in this area is Stephen King (yes, the famous author of horror and thriller books.) He's also authored a book about his writing process, and extensively discussed the difficulty of editing his own work.

He's known for quoting William Faulkner on this, and referring to the elimination of things you love from your writing as "killing your darlings."

The words and ideas an author's written are our darlings. We're greatly attached to them. But if the ideas don't fit — if they're not all the most important information that needs to be conveyed to keep that forward momentum — we have to kill them off. It's painful, but absolutely necessary.

As teachers, we're the same way with our lessons. They are our darlings. We stayed up until 2 a.m. gluing wiggly eyes onto construction paper or reworking a project-based-learning experience based on some idea we saw on Pinterest, and we are going to fit in that aspect of the lesson the next day if it kills us!

We'd rather kill ourselves than kill our darlings.

And before this analogy gets even more morbid, let's head the whole problem off at the pass by eliminating that over-planning. Do fewer things, so you can do the things that remain better.

Practice staying in that mindset all the time. When there's a fire drill or a snow day, don't just keep pressing forward with your original lesson plans afterward. You're not going to have time for everything, and you have to eliminate some learning experiences.

You may need to admit to yourself, "I'm just not going to be able to teach this as well as I would have liked," and start looking through your plans relentlessly for things to cut. I encourage you to do that right away rather than just continuing to get further behind.

You must ask yourself daily, *"What's the most impactful way to utilize our class time?"*

Then eliminate the good to make time for the best.

In doing this, you are shifting your mindset from that of the frazzled, rushed, over-scheduled teacher to the truly productive one.

People who struggle with productivity tend to add new tasks and responsibilities to what they're already doing, and ask themselves, "How can I fit all of this in? How can I possibly have time for all of this?"

Truly productive people look at a new responsibility and ask themselves, "Is this the best use of my time? And if so, what can I eliminate today in order to make time for this?"

Productive people are always analyzing whether something is really necessary, and whether it's really necessary right now. They're always re-evaluating their priorities and shifting tasks around.

Resist the urge to reinvent the wheel and chase shiny objects

As it becomes clear which activities and routines you want to streamline, your mind might be racing with all the things your students could finally have time to do. Projects! Design thinking! Collaborative experiments!

But if you're not quite sure what's the best use of instructional time, don't overcomplicate things. Start by figuring out what's already working, and do more of that.

What are the activities you're doing now which get great results? Which strategies have you tried that make you say, "Wow, the kids really understood that, and they were totally engaged"?

Maybe it feels scary to give up spelling tests or whatever else you know is not really the *best* way for students to learn and practice key skills. But what DOES work? What have you done with your students that DID improve their spelling or writing?

Also think about your favorite lessons to teach. Why do you like those lessons? What makes them so effective? Take a moment to analyze.

My favorite lesson was a hands-on math activity where the kids were moving things around instead of just working with pencil and paper. It created a lot of "a-ha" moments in which it finally clicked for the kids how division was related to making groups. We began with a teacher-led mini lesson, allowed students work at their own pace so they weren't waiting on everyone else, and had some valuable debriefing and reflection questions afterward. Students finished with an end product they were proud of and that gave them a real sense of satisfaction.

Were all of my lessons that awesome? Absolutely not. But by reflecting on the elements this one included which made it better than the others, I could find ways to do more of what worked. I could take one or two pieces of that lesson and repeat them elsewhere, and make some portions of the lesson a regular part of my instruction.

As you think back on your most effective lessons, look for patterns. Which lessons left you feeling the greatest sense of accomplishment — knowing that your kids understood the material, they were engaged, and you really enjoyed teaching them? What parts of those lessons can be repeated?

You can also think through some of your least favorite lessons. What are the activities and elements of your instructional day which you absolutely dread or cringe when you think back on?

Most of the lessons I didn't like to teach were either boring or confusing (or both). So, I could recall what I did during my most effective lessons and incorporate some of those strategies into the lessons that weren't working as well. I'd realize there needed to be more student choice, or a more thorough introduction to build background knowledge, or a better set of practice activities to help kids apply the ideas right away.

> *There's more to determining if a lesson is successful than seeing if kids can pass a test afterward. You've already got assessments to see if students have mastered the standards. The process I'm describing is about self-assessing the quality of your instruction and finding lessons that fit well with your teaching style.*

When you find an activity that works, you can repeat those types of experiences over and over. I used the same twenty-ish types of practice activities in many contexts, and only deviated from them when the subject matter lent itself to that (i.e. if I was teaching about moon cycles, obviously, we built models of the moon). For all the other skills and topics, I was simply picking and choosing from what I already knew was effective.

For example, gallery walks (also called chat stations) are one teaching strategy I've relied on a lot. Students work in small groups to walk around the classroom and respond to texts, questions, or prompts that I placed in various parts of the room. This activity is versatile, and naturally differentiated. It can be used with any topic. It gets kids moving around and collaborating. They love it, and it's minimal prep.

So, gallery walks are a go-to activity in my teaching "bag of tricks." If I want kids to think and talk about a topic, I don't need to spend an hour online looking for a clever new way to do it. I can simply write "gallery walk" in my lesson plans, and the next day, tell kids that's what we're doing and they immediately spring into action.

This means there's no wasted time reinventing the wheel on my weekends.

And, there's no wasted class time explaining what to do, setting expectations, practicing procedures, and creating new routines.

If lesson planning takes you way too much time, this is the way you want to plan the bulk of your activities. You can start with 4-5 strategies which you know are effective for your students, and add more slowly over time.

This doesn't mean that you can never look for something new to try. If finding fun activities is part of your "hobby-work" that you do in your free time, that's great! I'm simply saying you don't *have* to do it in order to be an effective teacher, and there are other ways to keep things fresh and interesting in your teaching.

I promise that repetition of activities will not bother the majority of your students — they're probably used to doing worksheets and testing for a large portion of the school day, so repeating an activity they actually enjoy and find meaningful will get you a positive response. (And if it doesn't, either the kids didn't find it that engaging to begin with, or it's been overused — just add something new to your repertoire, and keep experimenting.)

Young kids like predictability, and older kids don't find things nearly as repetitive as we might assume. After all, they have 5-8 different teachers each day, so they're getting a lot of variety in teaching styles and activities, anyway.

For kids of all ages, it can feel like a relief to come to class and know what is expected. Students like knowing how to be successful without thinking too hard about what the procedure is for whatever new thing the teacher is trying out that day.

So, don't allow yourself to fall prey to "shiny object syndrome" in which you're chasing trends and distracted by every new-to-you teaching idea. Of course you're missing out on some cool stuff. If you had a million years, you still wouldn't have enough time to teach every awesome lesson idea that's possible.

But you don't have to spend excessive time thinking about what you *could* be doing, if what you're *already* doing is working well for you and your students. Consider where your time and energy is best spent, and be intentional about what you prioritize.

Part Four

I ENSURE MY NEEDS ARE
MET TO PREVENT
OVERWHELM & EXHAUSTION

It's a well-known fact that teachers wear many hats. You play the role of secretary, nurse, social worker, counselor, actor, events coordinator, coach, detective, referee, and so on.

But there's another role that needs to be filled, and you might not even be aware of it.

Anytime a group of people have a huge goal with a lot of "moving parts," someone needs to be in charge of managing the complete process and tracking little details to ensure everything fits together. A project manager is one of the most valuable assets an organization can have.

She or he studies the vision from the person in charge and works backward to break things down into actionable steps. The project manager creates systems and determines who's going to do each aspect of the work, then assigns the tasks, oversees them, and ensures everything comes together at the end.

Guess who's the project manager of your classroom?

That's right. Your school or district leaders set the goals, but you're in charge of figuring out systems and daily procedures for getting kids from point A to B in their development.

In other words, someone in charge tells you *what* needs to be done, perhaps in excruciating, micromanaging detail. But *you* are the Project Manager, and you must figure out how to ensure that everything which is required actually happens.

Whether consciously or not, you're constantly asking yourself the questions of a project manager:

At what point in the schedule should each requirement be handled? How much time needs to be allotted to each aspect? What's the most efficient way to get each requirement completed? How does each new task fit in with the existing tasks? Which ones should be prioritized first?

And here's the kicker: a project manager's time should be focused primarily on *managing projects*. Seems obvious, given the job title.

That means a PM should be *delegating* the majority of the work: telling each team of people about their deadlines and keeping them on track, handing off one set of completed tasks to the next person in the chain, etc. The project manager is not supposed to be doing all of the work alone. The job would become overwhelming, and go well beyond the PM's scope of expertise.

As a teacher, though, you are not only managing all the projects (figuring out systems, routines, procedures, and making sure everything happens the way it's supposed to and according to the timeline), you are also responsible for completing the vast majority of the work, all by yourself.

You're given the learning standards and are responsible for orchestrating how to get every child to meet the standards. That's not a single task you can put on a to-do list and check off. It is an absolutely massive, ongoing *project*.

That's why lesson planning is so challenging and time-intensive: You have to design, research, manage, oversee, implement, and evaluate the project pretty much single-handedly.

And lesson planning is just ONE type of project you're in charge of. You also manage projects around behavioral issues, classroom design, organization, committee goals, action research, and more.

I share this not to depress you with the magnitude of your workload, but to help you understand why you're so exhausted every night.

No human could excel in all the areas a teacher is expected to master: lesson planning, lesson delivery, differentiating instruction, behavioral interventions, building rapport with kids, addressing students' socio-emotional issues, creating classroom routines, collaborating with colleagues, communicating with parents, implementing assessment, analyzing data, AND the five hundred other responsibilities of a teacher.

And yet you're not only expected to execute all those things well, you're also expected to plan, manage, and oversee all of them …

On top of managing the work of all your students!!!

If you dare try to simplify or take shortcuts in even 1% of this workload, you might be perceived as lazy or "not in the profession for the right reasons," so the responsibility for managing everything stays firmly on your shoulders.

And then you go home and repeat the process for all your personal and household tasks, planning and executing far too many things there, too. The obligation to make sure everything's running smoothly and everyone's happy and nothing is forgotten never ends.

> *I refer to this kind of emotional labor and mental load as "Project Manager Syndrome." It's where you feel responsible for planning and orchestrating every detail of your life and the lives of those in your care.*

I believe it's one of the most insidious forms of burnout, because we have trouble recognizing it in ourselves or explaining the stress to others. Many of the responsibilities don't seem very big on their own, so we feel like we shouldn't complain.

But it's the cumulative weight that's exhausting: the sheer number of items to keep track of.

There might be 30 or more things to oversee just in the minor details of your students' day:

Remember to send Sarah to the Speech Therapist at 10:15; get Ahmed to the nurse for his asthma medication at 11:30; give the homework assignment to LaShay right before lunch since she's leaving early; make sure Mario has the extra copy of the study guide his mom requested; print out the recommendation letter for Justine; have Chloe check the lost and found for the hat she can't find ...

No wonder your brain feels like it's on overload!

We're going to use this final section of the book to look for ways you can release yourself from some of these project management tasks by delegating responsibility to others.

We'll explore mindset shifts to help you ease the mental load you're carrying, so that your brain doesn't feel like a computer with 638 tabs perpetually open.

And, we'll uncover lots of practical ways that you're creating unnecessary work for yourself, so you can practice relaxing your standards and letting go of the need to oversee and control everything you're currently responsible for.

Don't get complacent, and assume you can skip the stuff around rest and self-care because it's just about taking bubble baths. Some of the most challenging work is at the very end of this book. We're going to uncover some subconscious beliefs about what you "have to do" in order to be effective in all of these roles you're playing, and the deeper reasons why you stay frazzled instead of prioritizing your needs.

It's only once you've identified and let go of your limiting beliefs that you'll be able to break free from overwhelm and exhaustion. You'll finally be able to give your mind a true rest from thinking about everything that needs to be done, and disconnect from your work and personal responsibilities.

Let's tackle this last part together now, so you'll be ready to create space in your daily routines for rest, recharging, and taking care of yourself.

10

Releasing yourself from perfectionism and unnecessary work

I hope it's obvious that the magnitude of your workload becomes even more overwhelming if you try to manage it while running on four hours of sleep and while completely lacking exercise, fresh air, and healthy food.

When you sacrifice so many of your own basic needs that you're left totally exhausted, the responsibilities begin to feel oppressive. You don't have the energy to show up the way you want to. That leads to guilt and underperformance, which causes you to overwork to compensate.

Deep down, you know that you'll do a better job at all your responsibilities when you're rested and rejuvenated.

But it's time for you to stop nodding along when people tell you that, and start actually living it.

Recognize that because you have a tremendously important and demanding job, you won't be able to do it even halfway right unless you take care of yourself and make sure your needs are met.

Would you want to fly in a plane with a pilot who's as exhausted as you are?

Would you undergo surgery with a doctor who's never had a moment to think or rest?

Of course you'd want them to get in a better head space before you go under their care. You'd protest if they insisted they were fine and wanted to push through anyway because there was too much going on and they couldn't stop to recuperate.

So how do you think that working harder and doing more could possibly be the way to meet all the expectations on YOU?

Let's clear away the limiting beliefs and habits that are keeping you from making sure your needs are met.

Any perfectionistic or controlling parts of your personality that are undermining your ability to rest and draw boundaries are going to get sorted out, so you can clearly determine how to do fewer things better.

Look for "third rails" that overcomplicate and add stress

An underlying problem beneath many of the perfectionistic tendencies we'll talk about in this chapter are the "third rails" we create for ourselves.

The third rail in an electrical system carries a high voltage, and is therefore untouchable. Every New Yorker knows that if you accidentally fall onto the subway tracks, part of your survival depends on avoiding the third rail.

I'll use the term here to refer to self-imposed rules that we consider untouchable. We make policies about the way things are supposed to work, and it feels dangerous and therefore impossible to consider any alternative. Our survival seems dependent upon leaving the third rail alone. We won't get close enough to examine our third rails, and if anyone else dares to try, they're going to get a shock!

The teachers I've had the hardest time coaching are the ones who have strong views about personal responsibility, which become like a third rail which is completely untouchable.

These teachers have very rigid beliefs about what they and other people are responsible for doing. They tend to be driven by the desire to "hold kids accountable" based on beliefs about what kids are supposed to do and how families are supposed to parent. They may hold privileged assumptions based on their own social norms, and spend a tremendous amount of time bemoaning "kids these days," as well as the poor morals and work ethic of society in general.

Teachers with a lot of third rails will create endless extra work for themselves in order to avoid looking closely at the rules they've created. They are often resentful of this extra work, but don't feel like they have a choice. After all, they're just doing "what good teachers do." Any less would be unconscionable, and a violation of their strong personal work ethic.

So, they'd rather spend an hour after school completing behavior referral paperwork than permit any student to "get away with" challenging their authority.

They'd rather create ten different versions of every test than risk having a student "get away with" cheating.

They'd rather stay up until midnight grading every piece of paper students touched than allow them to "get away with" not putting in 100% effort on every practice assignment.

The motive on the surface is concern for kids' well-being (*How else will they learn how to behave properly and be responsible adults?*). But there's usually a fear underneath of not being respected or taken seriously, and a strong need for others to conform to their ideals.

Since they cannot control students' home lives or force children to do what they are "supposed to," these teachers bear up under all the responsibility themselves.

For example, they may have a self-imposed policy of calling parents every time a student has incomplete work, because they believe that's part of their job as a teacher. They'll continue to call even when they know the parent will never respond, or will curse them out, or will hang up on them.

Why do they keep calling parents when they know they're not going to get a desirable result? Because calling parents is their third rail — it's a rule which is untouchable. Doing otherwise would feel like shirking their duties as a teacher.

They'll complain that they spend all their evenings contacting parents who don't back them up, but they'll never consider the possibility of shifting to an approach that actually works. It's the parent who's wrong, not them, and they're going to keep metaphorically banging their heads against the wall in the name of "doing what's right."

While the type of teacher I'm describing here is an extreme, we all create a number of third rails in our work and our personal lives. I encourage you to question those self-imposed beliefs and rules.

Consider the possibility that you do not have to immediately respond with a consequence anytime a student doesn't follow directions.

Consider the possibility that you do not have to give kids nightly homework in order to teach them to be responsible.

Consider the possibility that you do not have to assign a formal grade to every single assignment in order to hold kids accountable for their work and monitor their progress.

What you believe to be true about holding kids accountable might not actually be true, or it might not be the *only* way to do it.

Ask yourself, *Who says it has to be done that way? What would happen if I didn't do it? How can I find a more effective, efficient way to accomplish my goal?*

There is no aspect of your teaching or life that should be above questioning, and there are few absolutes in teaching. Most of our third rails have nothing to do with the things that are truly absolutes (such as "teachers should never dehumanize children") and far more to do with our own beliefs about personal responsibility.

Notice when fear and "what ifs" guide your decision making

I encourage you to particularly self-reflect on behavior management, because that seems to be the primary area in which many teachers (myself included) have found ourselves creating untouchable third rails.

Beware of overly harsh consequences in your discipline philosophy, and ways that you end up punishing yourself through the act of trying to teach kids a lesson. Notice when you apply punitive measures regardless of individual circumstance, and have no room for flexibility in your approach even when that approach is clearly not getting the needed result. These are signs that you may have created a third rail, and it's causing you to focus on "giving kids what they deserve" rather than understanding what they truly need.

Also beware of fear-based decisions around assessment, differentiation, and re-teaching.

Are there approaches you're using which completely burn you out and don't get the majority of kids where they need to be, yet you feel doing otherwise would be a betrayal of your commitment to kids? You might have created a third rail around assessment, so doing things differently would feel like being a lazy teacher or not caring about student progress.

This third rail becomes obvious whenever someone shares a strategy to help you streamline your grading practices, because you will immediately back away and justify your reasons for doing so. If I suggest that you record the minimum number of grades required by the district instead of grading every piece of paper your students touch, you might launch immediately into all the reasons why that's untenable:

- Kids wouldn't do the work (you have to motivate them to complete assignments and hold them accountable, and the ONLY way to do that is if they know there might be an F in the gradebook).
- You need to know your next teaching steps (and you couldn't possibly understand what students need by using existing data, observing kids during the lesson, and using exit tickets or another formative assessment).
- Students' grade point averages would be too low if you didn't take an excessive amount of grades (because there's no possibility of ensuring the grades you do record are an accurate measure of what students know and are able to do).
- Parents would report you to the principal (because they might somehow discover students occasionally did an activity just for practice that wasn't recorded in the grade book, and lose their minds over it).

These are all justifications for avoiding your third rails, and they prevent you from considering more effective, efficient ways to do your job. Not only can this mindset be harmful for kids, it will also prevent you from letting ANYTHING go.

IF YOU BELIEVE THAT A GOOD TEACHER MUST DO THIS ONE SPECIFIC THING OR NEVER DOES THIS OTHER APPROACH, THEN YOU WON'T BE ABLE TO QUESTION HOW THINGS HAVE ALWAYS BEEN DONE. AND IF YOU INSIST ON DOING WHAT YOU'VE ALWAYS DONE, YOU'LL NEVER GET BETTER RESULTS.

Also, notice when you've let a negative experience impact your entire teaching philosophy. Maybe one parent complained about a student writing a rude comment on their child's group work evaluation, so you now believe you can never do collaborative assignments or group assessment again, and peer editing is out of the question.

Or maybe one kid took a photo of your answer key, and now you think you have to rework your entire grading practice, ban cell phones from the classroom, and have all students and parents sign a contract to provide evidence they understand this is not allowed.

Don't build a third rail in response to one bad experience (or worse, in knee-jerk reaction to the potential for one bad experience). Stop creating unnecessary work for yourself because one student might take advantage or one parent might be upset.

Think about the framing you use in describing your policies. For example, some parents wouldn't like the idea of "kids grading their own papers." This doesn't mean you have to personally grade every assignment. It means you have to think critically about how to introduce and describe the practice: "We occasionally use self-assessment strategies as a research-based practice that allows students to have more ownership of their learning and receive immediate feedback on their progress."

When you're really thoughtful about your instructional choices, you'll have the research and confidence to defend them. A single disparaging comment no longer has the power to make you retreat back to the way things have always been done. You can make decisions based on what works best for you and your students, instead of cowering to what others might think.

Be quietly subversive, and make decisions from a place of determination: *I will figure out a more efficient, effective way to do my job. How could I make a different strategy possible for me, instead of focusing on all the ways that it couldn't work?*

Avoid superhero syndrome

Sometimes we create extra work for ourselves because of third rails, and sometimes because we are fearful about what might happen if we do things a different way. These can both be understood as forms of perfectionism: things have to be done to the particular standard in our minds and there is no other acceptable option.

We also create unnecessary work when we try to do everything alone, and control — rather than utilize — the people around us.

This is an especially tricky form of perfectionism, because many people think their problems would be solved if they had more help. An assistant (or a project manager!) would surely make a big difference. A clone would be even better.

However, those "obvious" game-changers might not be effective, even if they were possible.

In my business as an educational consultant, I have the ability to hire whomever I want, and to outsource any tasks I don't want to do. I started working for myself in 2008, and have had the financial viability to hire help since that very first year.

Sounds like a dream come true, right?

It might come as a surprise that I didn't start building a team until the fall of 2014. That means for *six years*, everything I was doing — consulting, instructional coaching, blogging, editing, speaking, publishing books, creating curriculum resources, responding to emails, social media, designing and fixing my website — literally *everything* was 100% my work and my responsibility.

I had the ability to get help. And yet I was a one woman show, by choice and as a point of pride.

The truth is that asking for help was just too scary. Doing everything myself gave me a feeling of self-sufficiency. It served as a set of armor, and I was totally unwilling to take the armor off.

How would anyone be able to understand exactly what I wanted? Surely no one would be able to do things as well as I could. I figured if I wanted things done "right," I would have to do them myself. There was no other possible way.

I was stunned to learn from entrepreneur Chris Ducker that my feelings were actually quite common. People who are unwilling to ask for help because they believe no one else can do things how they need to be done are said to have superhero syndrome.

This was a huge wake-up call. Chris' explanation struck me in a powerful way: If I'm the only one who can do something right, *then I'll be the one who will always be doing it.*

My heart sank with the realization that every task I was currently handling would be my responsibility forever, and things would never get less stressful.

And, everything I was hoping to accomplish would be limited by the scope of what I personally knew how to do and had the time and mental bandwidth to accomplish. If I didn't release myself from superhero syndrome, I'd have to scale down my goals.

That realization transformed my life and my business. For example, I never would have started my Truth for Teachers podcast if I'd had to learn audio editing and create all the transcripts, blog posts, and images myself. There simply wasn't enough time in my day to do all of those things alone. If wanted to make a bigger impact in the education field, I had to stop insisting on doing everything myself.

Even though your obligations and circumstances are different than mine, chances are good that you struggle in very similar ways with carrying too much of the workload. Maybe your superhero syndrome sounds like this:

- *I can't ask my partner to do the dishes because I don't like the way he loads the dishwasher.*
- *I can't ask my students to organize our class library because it won't look right if they do it.*
- *I can't co-plan with my teammates because they don't do things the way I want them.*

And on, and on, and on.

You don't exist as an island, and yet you've isolated yourself when it comes to getting things done. You've taken on the responsibility for tasks which the people around you are fully capable of doing.

You don't want to "owe" your coworkers, so you never ask them for anything.

You don't trust your family members to be responsible, so you bear the full weight of keeping the household on track.

You don't want to take time to train your students to organize and manage their learning environment and materials, so you stay on top of everything for them.

> *It's superhero syndrome that makes you feel like you are the only one who can do things the way they need to be done. Superhero syndrome convinces you that it's easier to do everything yourself than to train someone else or allow them to do things in their own way.*

And guess what — that puts you in the same boat I was in.

As long as you're the only one who can do things "right," you're the one who will always be responsible for doing them.

If you want to expand your capacity to achieve more or even just shorten your to-do list, you have to adapt the same mindset that I needed to adapt, and begin sharing the workload.

No, your family members, students, etc. will not be able to do things exactly like you do them. But 80% done by them is better than 100% done by you.

You may have to explain the task, train them, and get them started (the first 10%), and you might have to do the final 10% yourself to clean up any errors or put the final touch on things. But if the middle 80% can be delegated, that's 80% less work for you.

Even 40% done by someone else is better than 100% done by you. Don't allow your own standards for how things "should" be done keep you stuck in a place where you can never delegate or get assistance.

Let go of the guilt about asking (and paying) for help

As I shared, the idea of seeking out help from other people did *not* come naturally to me, and hiring people required a major identity shift. I grew up in a middle class home, with my father in the army and my mother primarily a homemaker since we moved constantly.

We weren't "the type of family who hired help" (whatever that means). I guess I was picturing people who sat around on yachts drinking champagne, and saw them as spoiled and lazy. Paying for help with household tasks didn't seem like something that regular people like us would do.

It took me years to figure out most folks have no qualms about hiring help when a pipe in the house is leaking (a plumber), or a fuse is continually blowing (an electrician), and so on. But if there is a task that someone in the household is capable of doing, we feel we should handle it.

Why waste money when we can do it ourselves? Who cares if it takes the entire day on Saturday and we're exhausted and sore afterward, as long as we got it done for free? It's a classic trap of valuing money more than time.

Certainly there may be instances when money is far too scarce, and time is the only currency even somewhat available. But it's the mindset that needs to be examined more than the budget.

Are we automatically looking for ways to save money at great expense to our time? Or are we consciously examining all options available to us and weighing the trade-offs carefully?

This is especially important for tasks that are considered "women's work" such as cooking, cleaning, and child care. Many women feel guilty about handing over those responsibilities to other people — even members of our own household — because we feel responsible for handling them ourselves.

As I learned to value my time as much as I value my money, I realized this was a short-sighted approach. As a single person living for years on a budget with a $35,000 teaching salary, I made the choice to begin hiring someone to clean my apartment every other month. Eventually it became once a month, which continues to this day.

Not having to deep clean your home saves time and physical energy. If you have children, it will free you up to enjoy activities with them. Anyone can clean your house, but only you can develop your relationships with people that matter to you. Think about the things that only you can do and that are your biggest priorities, and how you can outsource tasks that other people could do.

You don't necessarily need a lot of disposable income in order to outsource. Many grocery stores, restaurants, and dry cleaners offer free delivery services. Some car dealerships and repair shops will come get your car at no extra cost when it needs to be serviced, and then drop it back off at your home afterward.

You may be able to trade services (i.e. you watch a friend's kids every Friday night and she watches yours every Saturday night, or take turns driving and picking them up from various activities).

Think outside the box! What are some tasks that you dread doing and which consume a lot of your time, and how could you get help with part of those tasks in order to free up time for more meaningful things?

Some opportunities may be unaffordable or unavailable to you right now, and that's okay for our purposes here.

The most important thing is to release yourself from any thinking which implies you are lazy, wasteful, or self-indulgent if you don't try to do everything yourself. If you're a woman, know that you are NOT failing as a mom, wife, or any other label if you aren't 100% in charge of everything domestic.

When you truly believe that, you'll be looking for creative possibilities and alternative ways to handle your workload, instead of assuming how things are now is the only way it could ever be done.

If you noticed feelings of judgment arising when you read these suggestions ("I can't believe people do that, that's so lazy" or "that's something I could NEVER do, people like me don't have that kind of money"), sit with those feelings and examine them. Consider how changing your perspective on getting help could free up more time and energy, and think about the potential value of that time to your life.

Stop project managing every aspect of home and work

At the beginning of this section, I explained how a teacher's project management workload is often the most insidious energy-drainer. However, Project Manager Syndrome also tends to be pervasive in our home lives.

Numerous studies have shown that even when a husband and wife are employed full time, the woman still ends up doing the lion's share of household tasks. This holds true even when men report splitting the work evenly, perhaps because women take on tasks that their partners aren't aware they're handling and don't notice or care about.

In the book *Drop the Ball*, author Tiffany Dufu writes about women in our culture,

    We believe that whatever we can do better and faster, we should just do ourselves. The problem is that we believe we can do *everything better and faster, so everything ends up on our list ... Before someone else can take the reins, women have to release them first. When Lean In author Sheryl Sandberg encouraged women to 'make your partner a real partner,' we all thought, Amen to that. Then we went home and put in another load of laundry. That's because actually enlisting our spouses, co-parents, and other people in our lives to help manage the home requires more than delegating tasks. It isn't child's play — it necessitates a substantive shift in our beliefs and expectations.*

This shift means allowing other people to truly own part of the responsibility for keeping things running smoothly. You have to let go of control and stop expending emotional labor on "helping." You will still be exhausted if you keep track of other people's to-do lists, remind them to follow through, and carefully critique their work.

Intentionally "dropping the ball" empowers the people in your life to find their own approach for tasks which they complete independently, rather than waiting for your directions, reminders, and approval.

THE ULTIMATE GOAL IS NOT TO HAVE EVERYTHING COMPLETED THE WAY YOU LIKE IT. THE GOAL IS TO STOP CARRYING THE LOAD OF PROJECT MANAGEMENT FOR ALL THE WORK BY YOURSELF.

Tiffany Dufu refers to this process as moving from "imaginary delegation to delegating with joy." That's because often, the delegation process is done only in our minds.

We sometimes expect other people (particularly spouses/partners and coworkers) to handle certain things, and get mad when they don't.

Later, we discover they had no idea they were expected to take charge.

We might hear comments like, "Oh, I didn't see that" or "I didn't know it needed to be done" or "I thought you had it handled — why didn't you ask for help?"

Don't fall into the trap of being the project manager for every task at home and school, and allowing others to do nothing unless you coordinate all the logistics.

Don't train people to believe you've got it all under control and they should wait passively for you to ask for help if needed. You *always* need them, because overseeing every joint task and delegating part of it to them is not your responsibility.

Instead, you can decide how to share the workload up front. When you delegate with joyful release, you and the other person come to an agreement *in advance* about who will be in charge of each aspect of each task. The other person must then back off, and refrain from issuing reminders, asking repeatedly if it's done, nagging about how to do it, or criticizing how the task was handled.

I can admit that intentionally "dropping the ball" has taken a lot of experimentation in my own life, particularly in my marriage. My husband and I have tried all types of labor division, including splitting things 50/50 earlier in our marriage when it felt important to me that things be "fair."

To be honest, fairness didn't work nearly as well distributing tasks based on our personalities and strengths. Rather than aiming for 50/50, we now look for happy/happy, and try to find approaches that don't make either person feel frustrated or taken for granted.

We discovered over time, for example, that I'm faster with most things on the internet, so now I do the majority of the online tasks for our household. And since my husband is a face-to-face person and knows I hate running errands and making phone calls, he's usually in charge of those tasks.

This distribution of work may not be equal in any given day. I might be able to whip through all the online stuff in a few minutes, while he's stuck on the phone the whole morning and spending the afternoon fighting traffic on the way to the bank, dry cleaners, and post office.

But our household runs more smoothly when we each stay in our own lanes, do what we do best, and allow the other person to handle what they do best without interfering or micromanaging.

This process of "delegating with joy" can be tough for a person who is used to being in charge and has strong preferences about how things should be done. It's easier, though, if you focus on the freedom that comes from not having to oversee every aspect of your home and school work, rather than focusing on the discomfort of not having things done the way you like.

Create a self-running classroom by giving kids more responsibility

I've found that students are a greatly underused resource when it comes to delegation. In many classrooms, students are only helping out in minor ways, such as by erasing the board or holding the door.

But YOU don't have to be the one issuing constant reminders, tracking missing work, straightening up behind them, and so on.

No matter what age group you teach, your students can probably take on more responsibility for maintaining the learning environment, as well as responsibility for the learning itself.

The untapped potential of your students is there — you can see it every day at dismissal. The school day is over, and you're ready to collapse in the corner from exhaustion. Meanwhile the kids are bouncing off the walls, racing down the hallways, shouting to their friends, and basically acting the most energetic they've been all day.

Why? Because you were on your feet for the last seven hours, and the kids spent most of that time sitting down and watching you run yourself ragged. You were probably working much harder than your students. You completed more tasks than they did. You put forth more effort and concentration than they did. You carried more of the mental load of remembering everything that needs to be done.

You can change that by automating routine tasks in your classroom and delegating much of the workload to students.

Rather than looking around for something menial a child could probably do in order to feel useful, ask yourself, *"What tasks would actually transfer responsibility for a smooth-running classroom from me to the students?"*

Any regular classroom task which you want to be performed automatically without your direct supervision can be assigned as part of a job system. Think about which tasks wear you out, and how you can delegate the responsibility to kids who would enjoy helping. For example:

- **IT Team:** Troubleshoots when other students need help with devices; turns equipment on in the morning and off before dismissal; recharges laptops; installs software updates; ensures equipment like headphones are cared for and functional

- **New Student Trainer:** Acclimates new students to classroom routines; helps gather textbooks and needed materials; for them; shadows new students during their first day

- **Absent Student Helper:** Ensures materials are ready for students who are absent; briefly reviews content that was covered during the absence and answers questions

- **Paper Collector:** Organizes assignments that students have turned in to prepare them for grading (i.e. puts papers in number order or alphabetical order by last name, makes a note of any missing work)

Obviously the youngest students will not be able to do as many things independently, but if they keep their jobs for at least a week — if not a month — they'll be far more successful because that gives them time to internalize the expectations. You can also assign jobs to pairs of students so they share the responsibility and can help each other. You will need to give reminders at first, but then students will remember who's responsible for each job and they'll remind each other. Have them train the next student to do their jobs so that you don't have to oversee things as closely as the year continues.

If you're worried that older kids won't buy into the concept, present it as an actual job for which students fill out a short application. Students can be "fired" from their jobs if they don't do them well, and have opportunities to "quit" and apply for another type of job. For a job completed successfully, some teachers even issue "payment" in the form of homework passes, classroom bucks, extra credit points, permission to listen to music with headphones while working, etc.

Some secondary teachers have had good results with assigning ongoing jobs only to specific students who really want them. You might formalize arrangements that kids have initiated themselves. For example, if there's a pair of students who always makes sure your Chromebooks are plugged in, make an agreement with them to have full control over that responsibility. Or, list out the jobs that need to be done and have students volunteer, keeping the same jobs for the entire month, quarter, or semester to keep things simple.

Additional jobs can be assigned within the context of collaborative work. For example, when doing a project, have students self-appoint a "materials manager" for their group who gathers supplies and puts them away, a "reports manager" who ensures all paperwork is turned in at the end of the project, and so on.

Or, give simple tasks to students according to where they sit in the classroom. And at the end of the week, for example, all students in the front row (or Table 1, if they sit in groups) are responsible for shutting down the technology; all students in the second row or group make sure materials/books/other supplies are properly organized, etc.

When meaningful tasks are assigned and kids are entrusted with jobs that are essential to your daily routines, students become much more invested in remembering their tasks and doing them well. Classroom jobs will become a fundamental part of their day, which means that you no longer have to be the project manager for every single task.

Relax your standards for things no one else will notice

The real reason most of us don't give kids enough responsibility in the classroom or share the workload enough at home is not that we think other people can't handle it.

They *could* handle it, but only if we micromanage their work to make sure it's consistently up to our standards, and that feels like more work than doing it ourselves.

Here's what you need to remember. When you're the only one who's exhausted at the end of the day, and you're carrying the mental load of remembering everything for every person around you ... and when you're spending hours each week doing the same time-consuming tasks over and over, only to find your work is undone thirty minutes later and no one seems to care ...

It's time to *relax your standards to a level where no one else will notice but you.*

Our quest for perfection — that is, for things to match up to our own personal standards — keeps us from getting others to pitch in.

And we don't necessarily realize the problem is perfectionism. We might say, *"I don't need it to be PERFECT. I know they're not going to make it perfect. I just need it to be the way I like it."*

Of course, needing things to meet your standards and not accepting anything else is the definition of perfectionism. No one works off an arbitrary standard of perfection. We all define "a job well done" a bit differently.

And when you won't settle for anything less than what YOU think is just right, and when you can't let something go until it's exactly where you want it to be, you've created unrealistic standards. That means you're creating unnecessary pressure and work for yourself.

Perfect is the enemy of done. You have to shift from trying to get things "just right," and focus on making them be "just fine."

Examine the ways you are making tasks overly complicated and spending time and energy on things that aren't necessary.

Consider the work ethic you've been trained to internalize. Were you taught to always do your best and give 100%?

 THE REALITY IS THAT IT'S IMPOSSIBLE TO GIVE OUR BEST TO EVERYTHING, BECAUSE THERE ARE LIMITS TO OUR TIME AND ENERGY, AND NO LIMIT TO THE THINGS NEEDING TO BE DONE.

Perhaps more importantly: *not every aspect of every task is worthy of our full time and attention.*

Often the only person who notices or benefits in any measurable way from our effort is ourselves. It's our own standards we're trying to live up to.

If you can relax your standards for a task without anyone else realizing it, then your standards are probably too high. They might not even be standards you consciously set, but instead, things you have been conditioned to assume you have to do.

Let's take tidying up around the house as an example. The standard that your home be spotless or even just well-managed is a gendered expectation. We've been conditioned to believe that it's a reflection on how well the woman or women of the household "do their job."

If a single woman's home is slightly messy, she might avoid inviting people over, out of fear they'll think she "lives like a pig." She may apologize profusely for the three items which are out of place. Single men are less likely to have this concern, because society doesn't train them to correlate their identity and self-worth to how neatly they keep house.

If a woman is married and has children, she may feel a messy house shows she's not properly caring for her family (rather than concluding that her spouse and kids haven't been cleaning up after themselves.) The dirty house ultimately feels like her responsibility, because the dominant culture tells us the house is a reflection of her skills as a wife and mother. If others in her household don't care, she has to pull their weight, because she's the one afraid of looking bad if the house isn't clean.

There's a built-in excuse for everyone else to have relaxed standards. (*"You know how men are, what are you gonna do? Such slobs. Kids are so messy. Teenagers — ugh. They're impossible."*)

But there's no such saying for responsible grown women. If the house isn't in tip-top shape, it feels like a moral shortcoming, a heartless dodge around our most important duty.

This pressure we feel as women is not usually due to the men in our homes being incredibly clean and organized and demanding that we conform to their approach. The overarching expectations are set by the culture at large. Our standards as women may be high because we subconsciously tie our worth to the appearance and cleanliness of our homes (and classrooms), in a way that most men do not.

This conditioning is how we convince ourselves we need to do more than is necessary, and set the bar far higher than needed.

So, examine the standards you're setting in your home. Do you really need to vacuum as thoroughly and frequently as you do? Who said it has to be done that way? There are some people who clean their floors daily, and others once every few weeks.

The difference in their workloads is quite significant ... and ultimately, is the payoff worth the effort? Would the difference be perceptible and important to anyone but you?

If you're only doing a task frequently because YOU care about it (or think you should,) relax your standards.

If you're only doing a task yourself because no one else can do it the "right way", relax your standards.

The only standard for your home that's truly necessary is that it be sanitary enough not to pose a health risk, and tidy enough that you can find things you need (and put them back again) fairly easily.

What if you allowed a bit of dust or pet hair to sit for a couple more days? What if you allowed your family's attempts at mopping the floors to be good enough for you? What if you stopped using the cleanliness of your home as a measure of whether you're a good wife or mom and "have everything together"?

Relaxing your standards would probably leave your home looking basically the same to everyone else, and you'd end up saving countless hours by the end of the year. Look for ways to ease up on yourself and make your workload lighter.

What would it look like if it were easy?

I am a person who loves excellence, particularly in my work, and I frequently raise the bar much higher than necessary.

When I find myself setting unrealistic standards or over-complicating my tasks, there are two questions I rely on to help me find my way out.

The first question is attributed to Tim Ferriss: "What would it look like if it were easy?"

I know perfect is the opposite of done, and things will never get done if I insist that that they be perfect. So I ask myself all throughout the day, "What would it look like if it were easy or simple?"

This question gives me some distance from the problem and helps me think about how another person might approach the task, or the advice I'd give to someone else in my situation. I'm great at solving other people's problems, but it's much harder to solve my own!

Typically, the easy, simple way means to stop overthinking and over-complicating it, and take action.

So when you don't know what to pack for lunch and you're just staring in the refrigerator, ask yourself, "What would this look like if it were easy?" and you'll immediately know what the simplest solution is.

When your entire classroom is a wreck and you can't figure out where to begin organizing, ask yourself, "What would this look like if it were easy?" and you'll find yourself intuitively knowing to pick up the items you see right in front of you.

The other question that helps is: "Can I just …?"

This prompts me to think of a path forward that is so easy it requires basically no willpower, time, or energy. It's a great way to identify what's truly necessary.

Here are some examples:

- *I don't have time to clean out the cabinet like I wanted to, so can I just organize the materials for our upcoming unit, and do the rest later this month?*
- *I'm too busy to type out that nice summary of student learning for the parent newsletter this week, so can I just share a photo of student projects and encourage families to ask their kids about it?*
- *I can't spend time with my mom today like I hoped, so can I just call her on the way to the store?*
- *I can't take a nap like I planned this afternoon, so can I just sit for 5 minutes and rest?*

Don't wait to take action until you can do the task "just right." That will create overwhelm and cause you to keep putting it off.

Instead, ask yourself "Can I just" and see what your first thought is. It's probably the right one, and your efforts will be just fine.

Start with the minimum viable product (MVP)

Another way to release yourself from the trap of perfectionism is to think about the MVP. This is a term from the business and marketing world, and refers to the Minimum Viable Product.

Take a cell phone company, for example. They know that a new phone isn't perfect when they release it.

As long as it's not going to catch on fire, that's fine. A few bugs are expected. They're not going to really understand what works and what doesn't until they get it in the hands of real people. They release the MVP to their users, and then they iterate, based on user feedback.

In our industry as teachers, the MVP principle works like this: You get a lesson plan or activity just to where the core features are in place, and you deploy it. Then you come back and add more features later, based on feedback from your users — your students.

Let's say you're creating a presentation for a lesson. Figure out how much time you can realistically allot to the task, and stick to it. Set a timer for 45 minutes and discipline yourself to create an MVP in that time period.

Enter all the text into the slideshow first. You now have a minimum viable product! If — and only if — you have time left over, you can make it look cute and add the cool interactive features you envisioned. But do not spend your entire weekend playing with the fonts and looking for graphics. You have created a boundary around your time for this project, and you must stick to it.

Use the MVP with your students. Then make notes for yourself about how the lesson went. You'll probably realize that you needed to switch things around and add more information, and a lot of the awesome ideas you had for making the presentation incredible were either unnecessary or different from what your kids actually needed.

These were things you never would have figured out if you hadn't taken the leap and presented the minimum viable product to your users — the students.

> *A minimum viable product is not about a minimal product. It's recognizing that you're going to have to iterate and revise based on students' needs.*

It's not going to be "perfect" until you've tried it with your kids and learned from what works and what doesn't!

Before you use that presentation again with another class, you can set aside another realistic time period for improving it. Over time, the presentation will become amazing. You'll be able to copy existing text and design settings from that presentation to make more presentations, meaning that each slideshow you create will be better than the last AND you'll be able to make them faster.

It all starts with a minimum viable product. First make it work, then make it work better.

Practice shifting your mindset from designing the learning *for* kids to designing the learning *with* kids.

You can apply this MVP principle to every aspect of your life:

- What would it look like for you to live in beta mode instead of expecting yourself to have all the right answers before you begin?
- What if you no longer expected yourself to function with no errors at 100% capacity at all times?
- What if you gave yourself permission to be constantly iterating, and looking for ways to make things better, instead of expecting things to be perfect from the start?

The MVP principle frees you to focus on the most essential elements of what needs to be done, and improve and expand on your work over time.

Every YES means a NO to something else

A final strategy to help you stop overcomplicating your work is to remind yourself of the time and energy that's at stake.

Every time you say yes to unsustainable personal standards, you are saying no to something else: your health, your family, your hobbies, and so on.

But when you say no to unnecessary work, you can say yes to an infinite number of other things that matter to you.

What could you say YES to if you said NO to perfectionism?

We all have our little hang-ups and certain things that we insist be done a certain way. I encourage you to take the risk and consider what else could be possible if you released yourself from unnecessary standards.

For example, you might spend hours every week searching online for learning materials, and then spend several more hours re-creating and adapting every single thing you found because none of them were exactly what you wanted. Though part of you enjoys it, you also know this habit is keeping you from having adequate downtime in the evenings.

Think of more innovative approaches — there has to be a better way! What if you:

- Split the task of curating good ideas with another teacher using shared Pinterest boards?
- Used a co-worker's activities for one class and let her use yours for another?
- Purchased a few ready-to-use materials that are higher quality than the freebies and don't need adaptation?

- Used fewer pre-made, teacher-directed activities and did more student-directed projects?
- Reused the same materials from last year and simply adapted your delivery?
- Created an MVP instead of an elaborate activity, and developed it over time with student input?

I hope you can see there are many possible approaches here, and *"spending hours searching online for ideas and adapting them every night"* is only one of them. It is not a necessary part of your job.

If you had an unlimited amount of time and energy, you could create all students' learning materials from scratch. But if you don't have time for everything else in your life because of this quest for "perfect" activities, it's time to relax your standards to a level where no one else will notice but you.

Think about the trade-offs you're making. Every time you say yes to reinventing the wheel, you're saying no to all the other tasks that are on your plate, which means that to-do list is going to keep growing longer.

You're also saying no to self-care, exercise, relaxing, sleep, and hobbies. This means you're less likely to have the focus and energy you need when implementing the lesson, and a terrific lesson doesn't mean much when the instructor is cranky and exhausted.

Your students need *you* to be at your best far more than they need the best lesson.

So when you find yourself trapped in a mire of perfectionism where you know you need to let things go, consider the opportunity cost and choose the better option. Ask yourself: *What would I be doing if I weren't doing THIS?*

11

Getting clarity through practices of rest and recharging

I used to think that if I didn't collapse into bed at night feeling completely exhausted, that meant I hadn't pushed myself to work to my full potential.

If I had the energy to do *just one more thing*, I felt obligated to do it. I did not feel a sense of accomplishment unless I'd expended every last drop of energy I had.

Then my husband and I visited Soufrière, a small town in the south Caribbean island of St. Lucia. Our plan was to relax for a few days and celebrate our anniversary, and St. Lucia turned out to be the perfect place.

I could see firsthand that the "cult of busy" did not exist in the same way it did at home. Folks would stop whatever they were doing to converse with people driving past. No one seemed frazzled or hurried or stressed by a schedule they needed to keep. Things happened when they happened. Just about everyone we saw made time for interactions with others, and lived in closer connection to the land.

I had that feeling at the end of the trip that so many Americans do after visiting other countries: *I wish I could be this laid back all the time. I wish this was the normal pace of life at home.*

But something clicked for me during that trip. I did some serious reflection on why I'd allowed the pace of my life to become so hectic.

When and how did total exhaustion become my standard for a productive day?

Why had I chosen to fill so much of my downtime with more productivity instead of allowing time for just *being*?

It finally sunk in that much of the hurried pace of life I took for granted is simply a cultural norm. It's not universal. It's not "just how life is." Millions of people all over the globe — across many cultures and continents — have a very different pace of life.

And that meant I could choose something different for myself.

If we take an honest look at our mainstream norms in the U.S., it's clear that most of us consider it a badge of honor to be busy all the time. We judge one another's importance by how much we get done and how many people are depending on us to accomplish things.

Consequently, a person who dares to spend half an hour watching a TV show without multitasking is seen as wasting time. They're not *accomplishing* anything.

> But if you never let yourself relax without also getting something done at the same time, that means you're never truly relaxing. It also means you're sabotaging your own ability to perform at a peak level the following day.

Our bodies are not made for nonstop productivity. Being constantly on the go keeps you from having the energy needed for what matters most. The time and attention you need for priorities gets spread out among too many areas, and your overall impact is limited.

But even more critically, the constant need to be "doing things" leaves you with no time for getting clarity on what's most important.

Your priorities, goals, and legacy will only come into focus when you give yourself space to think about them. Carving out time for rest and recharging is fundamental.

Time you enjoy wasting is never wasted

When I returned home from St. Lucia, I was determined to break the cycle and create change in my life, but I knew that a more relaxed pace would be hard for me. So, I decided to try scheduling downtime into my calendar.

Yes, *scheduling* downtime — don't laugh.

8-9 p.m. was now going to be set aside for reading and watching my favorite shows with my husband on our DVR. No checking email or wiping down the kitchen counters while watching. I'd be doing nothing but immersing myself completely in a story.

This experience was a game changer. I realized that having scheduled downtime freed me from the guilt of doing "nothing" and the feeling that I should be tackling my to-do list, since watching the show was one of the tasks I'd written down and intended to complete that day. I had total permission to relax for an hour, and that frantic part of me felt a little calmer with the understanding that at 9 p.m., I could get back into motion if I wanted to.

This habit also motivated me to work more quickly and efficiently. I knew I needed to stop whatever I was doing right at 8 p.m., so I didn't have time to waste. I worked with intention to get things finished around the house, and then I relaxed with intention.

Over time, I got more comfortable with the feeling of not being productive, and stopped judging my own success by that measure.

My previous habit had been running through a mental list at the end of each day, thinking about all the things I got done so I could judge my "success" and accomplishments. This would leave me feeling stressed about all the incomplete tasks, and tomorrow's to-do list would run through my mind as I tried to sleep.

But I learned to stop thinking about what I did or didn't get done, and instead ask myself, *What did I enjoy today? What did I do that brought me happiness and fulfillment?*

What I enjoyed is just as important as what I got done. Happy hour with my girlfriends? Integral to decompressing. Five minutes on the porch, just breathing fresh air? Critical to my well-being. Both of those things were just as important as getting to inbox zero with my email, because they meant I actually stopped to be present and enjoy my life.

I discovered there's a big difference between wasting time and being unproductive. When I intended to get work done but ended up watching TV to avoid the task, I felt annoyed with myself. That was wasting time, because I didn't get any real enjoyment from it.

But when I put everything else to the side and allowed myself to be present in an intentional moment of relaxation, it felt really, really good. I realized that I *was* being productive by relaxing. After all, I was accomplishing something that was important to me: bonding with people I cared about and taking time to enjoy life.

If relaxation is a priority for you, then it's worthy of dedicated time in your schedule on a regular basis. Once you learn how to enjoy downtime and are comfortable with not being productive, you won't have to schedule it anymore.

I'm now at a place where I can create a realistic to-do list for the day and close the laptop guilt-free when it's time to be done.

I don't feel like I have to keep working until exhaustion, because I know stopping before that point will give me time to enjoy my life AND have more energy to be productive the next day.

I realize now that I can't be successful in all the "doing" if I'm not also making time for "being." So, I'm no longer measuring my success by how much I got done in the day. Enjoying my downtime is just as important to me, and just as integral to my well-being.

Shift your self-worth away from accomplishments

Changing your own definition of a successful day might require you to unpack the belief that hard work is a moral necessity and a defining mark of good character. That's been a core American value since the time of the Puritans.

Think of the adages which have been passed down for generations: *The price of success is hard work. Success comes to those who work for it. If you work hard, you can be anything you want.*

In reality, hard work and success don't fit together that neatly. You can work like a maniac, but if you're not focused on the tasks that help you get ahead, then you're just spinning your wheels. There are many people working nonstop but making little progress toward their goals.

And, there's no guaranteed connection between hard work and financial or career success. There are people who work incredibly hard at three or four jobs, yet never make enough money to be considered middle class. There are also people who spend little time working yet live quite comfortably: perhaps other people in their family have made enough money to support them, or they have jobs that pay well without being time-intensive, or they live simply with few material possessions.

WORKING HARDER DOESN'T MEAN YOU'LL GET WHAT YOU WANT, AND GETTING WHAT YOU WANT DOESN'T MEAN WORKING HARDER.

The collective obsession with a strong work ethic is relatively new in the perspective of human history. Our first ancestors are believed to have only worked a few hours a day. Time for rest was natural and valued for many generations, because they only had to produce what was needed to survive.

Subsistence living doesn't require 24/7 productivity. Producing goods and services for the profit of others does.

The industrial revolution sped up the shift toward this out-of-balance lifestyle that we know today. When electricity was invented, work could easily begin before sunup and continue after sundown. The harder people worked, the more profits could be made for their employer. It benefited factory owners to enforce a work ethic that pushed people to their limits physically, even if they were barely being paid enough to survive.

Sound familiar?

In teaching, this work ethic manifests through the belief that you have to put in more hours to prove your good character.

Educators who arrive at school early, stay late, and bring work home on the weekends are perceived as hard workers and more committed to the success of their students. Teachers who arrive just before the first bell and leave at 3 p.m. are side-eyed. You can't possibly do a good job as a teacher without working endless unpaid hours, right?

And yet closer examination doesn't bear this theory out. We all know teachers who stay at school until dinner time, but they're passing out worksheets from 1982. And, we all know teachers who are extremely good at what they do, yet never seem to stay much later than required.

> Your effectiveness is not about working long hours — that only gives you the appearance of being dedicated or a hard worker.
>
> Your effectiveness is based on doing things that make the biggest impact for kids. There is no direct correlation between the number of hours you work and your teaching effectiveness.

We have to unlearn the conditioning that tells us otherwise. We have to disassociate hard work with success, and recognize that work doesn't have to be difficult or all-consuming in order to get results. Otherwise, if something doesn't *feel* like hard work, we'll assume we didn't do enough … and if we're not getting the desired outcome, we'll assume the problem is lack of effort and press on until exhaustion.

We also have to stop valuing the appearance of hard work and how much we produce as a measure of our worth. Prioritizing your own needs is not lazy, it's wise. You don't have to get things done or create results for other people in order to be valuable as a human being.

Who you are at your core is valuable apart from what you do. So, you must consciously choose to stop measuring your success by how much you get done. Instead ask,

Am I taking care of myself?

Am I doing the things that matter most in life?

Am I living out my purpose and taking joy in that?

Am I present in the small moments that add up to a fulfilling life?

Am I enjoying and making the most of my experience on this planet?

These kinds of questions shift your focus away from doing, and into being. You can change your definition of success and the way you measure the quality of your days. In fact, when you understand the reciprocal relationship between enjoyment and accomplishment, rest and productivity, stillness and action ... then you can begin to feel good about opening up space in your life for both.

The myth of giving 110% and "doing whatever it takes"

The expectation for teachers to give their all for students during the school day *and* be willing to work for free during their evenings and weekends is often framed as "giving 110%."

This has always puzzled me. How can you give more than 100% of yourself? Where is that extra 10% coming from? And even if you "just" give 100%, what would you have leftover for the rest of the things that matter in life?

The other framing we often hear is that teachers must do "whatever it takes" to help their students succeed. The implication is that you don't have permission to stop until every child is successful in every way, and if you take a moment to rest and care for yourself while a student is not yet mastering standards, then you're not giving 110%. You're not doing whatever it takes.

Many of us drive ourselves toward an early grave by this insistence on perpetual giving. We carry the emotional burden of not letting any student be left behind. We're working triple time, trying to put forth energy on behalf of students who give very little in return and students who are weighed down by poverty, under-resourced communities, and systemic issues we're trying to compensate for.

And yet we feel like it's *our fault* when the kids don't succeed, because we could have done more. We could have always done more.

The pattern repeats every school year with a new group of kids. We give more of ourselves than is even possible to give, driven by the belief that *we have to do whatever it takes.*

My friend, there is an operative word in that phrase that I think most of us miss.

WE have to do whatever it takes. WE, as in the school community.

Not YOU. Not one individual teacher who's constrained by the bureaucracy of a school system that never does "whatever it takes" when it comes to proper funding and staffing.

We have to do whatever it takes. We, as a nation, have to keep addressing the big issues that are holding our kids back. We, in our local communities, have to offer support, services, funding, compassion, and love.

This cannot all be on your shoulders as one person. That's too big of a weight for you to carry, and you will not succeed on your own.

You are not responsible for carrying the burden that's supposed to be assigned to parents, extended family, your colleagues, your principal, your superintendent, or the government. You're not even responsible for carrying the burden that's assigned to students. You can't do the work for them, you can't force them to learn, and you can't magically make them more invested in academics.

The only part of the teaching process you're responsible for is your own. And to walk in that truth, you have to first understand what you're responsible for, and then learn how to draw boundaries when anyone (including yourself) gives you a guilt trip about not doing enough.

Knowing what is "enough" to give each student is about accepting that there is always something more you could be doing to help. You could do 100 things for a student, but will still carry that nagging feeling that 110 things would benefit them even more. And you'd probably be right.

One way out of this trap is to look at what is sustainable for you and what's most beneficial for students. Let those be your two guiding principles.

So you might think to yourself,

> *I can't stay at school until 7 p.m. because then I'm not taking care of my health, my family, or the things that need to be done at home. I can stay two hours to work after school today, and that's it. Knowing that I have those two hours, what can I do that will benefit students the most? I can't do it all, so where should I channel my energy to have the greatest impact?*

When you feel resentment building because you're giving too much of your time (or focusing too much on a handful of kids and not enough on the rest of the class), trust your intuition. Follow that feeling that says:

> *I have done enough. I have a finite amount of time and energy for my students, and I cannot devote such a huge amount to just this one student or problem. I have to think about what I can do that will benefit my class(es) the most, and concentrate on that.*

I guarantee that you will feel guilt when you choose to create those boundaries. But remind yourself of the alternative. You can work yourself to the bone for students and burn out, or you can find balance which will allow you to stay in the profession and keep helping kids for years to come.

Those are the choices. You can't do both. Say NO to one thing so you have time and energy to say YES to something bigger.

LET THE VERY THING THAT IS CREATING GUILT ABOUT NOT DOING ENOUGH (YOUR PASSION FOR HELPING KIDS) BE THE VERY THING THAT GIVES YOU PERMISSION TO PACE YOURSELF.

You want to keep making a difference in students' lives for years to come, so you have to think about what's sustainable for you. Manage your energy. You want to get to the end of this race and know that you ran it well. So, treat teaching like a marathon, not a sprint.

Know and respect your own limits each day

Here's what this mindset looked like for me on a daily basis. I didn't make it overly complicated. I just gave of myself until I hit a point where I knew I'd be tired, resentful, and impatient with my students the next day if I did any more.

The breaking point was different each day, and it had very little to do with hours worked. It was much more about emotional labor and energy expenditure.

On the days when students are less demanding and things flow smoothly, you can give more, and you can work longer.

And sometimes dealing with tough issues will wear you out very quickly. So, do what you feel capable of doing that day, and then stop and take care of yourself.

There's no benefit in pushing past the point of what you know is sustainable, because you're just going to be worn out tomorrow. You'll snap at the kids, take shortcuts in your teaching, and undo all the good work you did today.

Experiment with choosing your stopping point based on what's going to set you up for success the next day.

You might think to yourself,

I could knock out those last few emails tonight, but if I stop working after dinner, I'll sleep better and wake up earlier and with more energy. I need 100% of my brain power for the lessons I'm teaching in the morning, and I'm not willing to risk compromising that for some non-essential emails tonight. I'm going to give myself permission to just chill out for the rest of the evening.

Remember, the goal is not to do everything you *can* do each day, but everything you *should*. More is not better.

Also remember that you are not responsible for trying to fix every problem, nor should you attempt to on your own.

Your students' success is not wholly dependent on what you do or don't do for them. You are one teacher out of many in their lives. You are one influence out of many. Your 10 months together are a very small part in the grand scheme of everything your students will experience and learn.

Do what you can to make a positive difference, but always stay focused on the goal of supporting the kids, not trying to "save" them.

When you start to hit a wall of resentment, it's okay to draw boundaries. Trust yourself to know what is enough each day.

Understand how to replenish your energy levels

As you begin to monitor your energy levels and release yourself from the obligation of always giving 110%, you'll be able to recharge in a way that wasn't possible before.

With the old mindset, you'd only be able to rest once everything was done. If you had energy left to do something for someone else, that meant you hadn't given 110% and needed to keep working.

But now, you can train yourself to believe that rest is a crucial part of your work, not the payoff you can only enjoy once the "real work" is complete.

 YOU DON'T HAVE TO WAIT UNTIL EVERYTHING ELSE IS DONE BEFORE YOU REST: YOU CAN REST SO THAT EVERYTHING ELSE CAN GET DONE.

Rest and relaxation work in a reciprocal way with productivity. Many people think rest is the *opposite* of getting things done, but it's actually the *catalyst* for it.

A lack of rest slows down your thinking. Coming up with solutions to problems is harder. Even the simplest tasks can feel like torture when you're exhausted and have nothing left to give.

So in practical terms, this means rest should be one of the highest priorities on your list. It's something you should set aside time for daily and nightly, regardless of how much work you did or didn't get done.

> *Rest takes up time, but it gives us more energy, and energy is one of our most important resources. In some ways, energy is even more important than time, because unlike time, energy does not automatically replenish itself each day.*

Every day that you're alive, you are given more time. You have another 24 hours to utilize. But you're not necessarily given more energy each day. You don't wake up with more energy unless you've done something previously to replenish it — unless you've taken care of your body and mind, and allowed yourself time to recharge.

Keep in mind that rest does not necessarily mean physical rest, although that's important, too. *It's also about creating space for mental rest from WORK.*

It can mean establishing a time of day — even if it's just a few minutes — in which you do not pressure yourself to accomplish anything or solve problems or even think about your responsibilities.

You'll perform at your optimal level when there are moments for rest and re-energizing peppered throughout your day. Rather than using them as a reward to save for when all tasks are done, think of ways to have moments of rest as soon as you start your day, and return to them over and over.

Maybe that means taking a few moments in the morning to meditate, do some easy stretches, or listen to a soothing song that allows you to transition gently from sleep to the demands of the day. Your moments of rejuvenation might come from listening to an audiobook in the car, or a few minutes midday of totally focused connection with someone you love.

All of these little habits add up to a lifestyle that is meaningful and fulfilling, rather than a race to finish as many things as fast as possible.

Also consider how you can create longer blocks of time for meaningful activities. When you're exhausted, it's natural to just crash on the couch to watch a show or scroll through some social media posts. And yet these activities are only satisfying in smaller doses. An hour of TV is fun; spending your entire evening, every evening, just staring at a screen creates an entirely different feeling.

Most of us can think of other activities which would leave us feeling more energized afterward. We have hobbies we'd love to spend more time on. We'd like to go for a bike ride or check out a festival, and often end our weekends wishing we'd made the effort to get up and do something more fun.

It's ironic that some of the things that replenish our energy levels the most also require a bit more energy to get started. You've got to set up all the supplies for crafting, or get dressed and drive to another part of town to participate in an activity with friends. And because we don't have any energy, we default to the easiest form of "self-care" instead. Wine. Chocolate. Instagram. TV.

In her book *168 Hours*, Laura Vanderkamp states that when people say they want more time, what they really mean is they want more memories. She shares that time seems to slip by so fast because we're not doing anything memorable.

Though it takes more energy to plan a fun outing than to just relax at home, those evenings at home all run together in your mind afterwards. The time seems to have disappeared because there's nothing to help you distinguish between the days.

Adding in more memorable events — even short, simple ones — will help you feel like your time was used to its fullest. Think about how you could use your time in a way that will be more memorable than what you're doing now.

You can start small: try to attend one event each week (or even each month) that requires a bit more effort but ultimately leaves you feeling satisfied, happy, and energized.

Stop feeling frazzled by reducing stimulus and seeking out silence

Imagine you're listening to the radio while driving on a rainy night, and visibility is poor. You realize you're having a hard time seeing where you're going, and — oops, did you miss that turn?

What's the first thing you do in that situation? Many of us will turn the music down, and hush everyone else in the car.

Doing so might seem silly.

How is turning off the music going to help us see better?

But we seek silence instinctively, because our brains are sending the signal that our attention has been split.

The quiet doesn't help us see where we're going. It helps us think better. We need to concentrate on not crashing or getting lost, and that means we need as little outside stimulation as possible: no music, talking, or even thinking about other things. We need to fully attend to the task of driving.

Your brain is sending you that same signal when you feel overstimulated or frazzled in other contexts. When all your students are chattering at once and trying to get your attention, you need to follow that period with a time for quiet and stillness. Your brain has been on overload, and it needs a break.

Many of us rarely give ourselves that break from stimulus at any point in the day. We may not have any moments of total silence when we can be alone with our thoughts.

It's hard to manage that with our busy schedules, of course.

But stimulus is also addicting, and we don't know how to function without it.

We'll say we want a few minutes of peace and quiet ("Can I just have two minutes in which no one's asking me to do anything?" or "Can I get ten minutes for myself?"). And yet anytime we have a few extra minutes, we immediately look for something else that needs to be done so we can fill up that time.

We'll reach for our phones and start looking for information to process. We actively find more things to do, watch, read, or listen to.

We'll leave the TV or music on for background noise, to the point where it feels strange to have silence in our homes or cars.

We never allow ourselves that mental break. Any free time in the day becomes an opportunity to either process more stimulus or do a random bunch of tasks (that were NOT on our list of priorities for the day), which keeps us in that energy-draining, high alert mode.

Our bodies were not built to handle the amount of light, noise, and information we constantly receive in the modern age. There's an unprecedented number of things competing for our attention, and the brain power we need for concentration is expended trying to process background noise. The sheer volume of stimulation weakens our decision-making abilities and wears us out more quickly.

I don't think we fully understand yet as a society what the ubiquity of cell phones is doing to our brains, in regard to both our ability to concentrate and our ability to mentally decompress.

People can call, email, or message us with demands and questions at all times of the day or night, and we receive them no matter where we're at. Our activities and thought processes are always interruptible, whether we're on a romantic date, traveling on vacation, or grieving loss at a funeral. Rarely do we go more than a few hours without checking our phones to see what requests have piled up in the short period of time we tried to disconnect.

This is normal, but normal is not synonymous with healthy, and our mental well-being is too precious to accept the status quo.

We can't wait for the world to quiet down.

We have to set our own boundaries, and create limits on how much information we are willing to process and how much of our day we will spend doing it.

I think it's true that some people need more recovery time and breaks from stimulus than others. And it's harder to get that break for some people, depending on where you live and what season of life you're in. But the noisier your environment typically is, the more important it will be for you to intentionally seek out times where you have less stimulation.

You can begin this process by practicing mindfulness. Leave the radio or TV off and notice how that feels. It might seem uncomfortable if you're used to it being on, but observe how it feels later. Are you able to get things done more quickly and with fewer distractions? Are you able to make decisions more easily? Do you feel less stressed afterward?

Practice enjoying silence, and allow moments of it throughout the day: before the first bell rings, during your lunch break, right after dismissal, in your car on the way home, while you're preparing (or eating) dinner, and so on. Just a few minutes of relishing the silence and concentrating on your breath can re-center you. It can give your brain a break from constantly processing so much information.

You can train yourself to tolerate stillness, let your mind wander, and rest. Your brain already knows what to do during those times. That's why your best ideas come to you in the shower, while walking in the fresh air, or while driving on an open road. These are moments when you have fewer distractions and stimulus, and your mind can open up to new possibilities.

You can create more opportunities like that in your life.

Imagine what would happen if you were to seize those small opportunities for rest, relaxation, and self-care throughout the day instead of squandering them with your phone.

Imagine what could be possible if you stopped trying to fill every moment with something productive, and lived as if you truly believe that rest is one of the most important things you can do.

12

Restoring balance and incorporating daily self-care habits

Is work/life balance actually possible?

Should that even be my goal when I love my work and don't want to create a defined cut-off?

How would I even begin to separate my work from the rest of my life, when being a teacher is who I am?

I think both balance and self-care are terms which are so overused (and misused) that they've become almost meaningless for many people.

Our focus in this final chapter is to unpack some myths and misconceptions, so you can tap into the real power behind these concepts.

We're going to get very specific about what balance looks like for you, and what type of self-care you personally need.

Generalized advice like "go to bed earlier" and "eat healthy" is not enough. You already know you should be doing those things, and they just become more stuff to feel guilty about not doing.

The practice of having true balance and regular self-care is centered on being mindful and in tune with your own needs.

It's about recognizing your breaking point and nurturing yourself before you get there.

It's about allowing yourself moments of presence and awareness in your body, mind, spirit, and emotions, instead of rushing around trying to accomplish more things.

It's about understanding what you need in order to thrive, and prioritizing those needs instead of only working to meet other people's expectations.

Self-care does not require you to buy things or surround yourself with luxuries. Commercialized self-care is mostly about self-indulgence. Enjoy it if you'd like, but understand that it's not integral to your well-being.

Coming home after work and collapsing on the couch with a pint of ice cream is not self-care, either. That's self-comfort. It feels good in the moment, and it's fine to do sometimes.

But real self-care is actually good for you. It's an act of caring rather than comforting yourself or indulging in pleasure that might not be particularly healthy.

Self-care acts are things that you want to regularly build into your life because they help you maintain a sense of balance.

You already know the old adage that you can't pour from an empty cup. The tricky part is to turn it from a truism into a life principle: to stop just agreeing with it, and actually live it. The way to do that is through defining balance for yourself and creating habits of self-care on a regular basis.

Figure out what work/life balance looks like for you

Many people hold the belief that work/life balance is impossible. And I agree, if the definition is giving equal, balanced time to everything that's important and feeling "in balance" at all times.

I define balance a bit differently.

For me, it's like standing on top of a ball or beam. If you've tried that before, remember the sensations you had while attempting to stay balanced.

Your instinct is to hold completely still, get yourself in position, and then DON'T MOVE AT ALL, so you'll be able to stand there, perfectly balanced, indefinitely.

But think about how balancing actually works. It's impossible to hold completely still when you're standing on a round ball or a thin beam. You have to be very present with what you're experiencing, and make small adjustments constantly: lean a little forward, now a little bit backward, now an involuntary wobble to the right, and an intentional shift to the left to counter it, and so on.

No matter what you do, eventually you will still get off balance and fall. So you regroup, get back up, and resume the act of balancing once again.

 BOTH PHYSICAL BALANCE AND WORK/LIFE BALANCE ARE ACTIVE PROCESSES — THEY REQUIRE CONTINUAL OBSERVATION AND ADJUSTMENT.

Don't fight that by trying to attain balance once and for all, and then getting frustrated when you're thrown off. Accept that balance requires monitoring yourself, and shifting around constantly. It's all part of the process!

There will always be new things that get added to your daily life and things that get removed, and any addition or removal will throw off your existing balance. All you have to do is look for balance *now*.

You might be a little wobbly, and you might fall off altogether. Just engage actively in the process of balancing, and be ready to adjust. Whatever you're doing now won't keep you balanced forever, but trust that you'll know the next move when the time comes.

Identify your "Core 5" for balance and well-being

Having a balanced life doesn't mean giving balanced time to everything. You can't divide up your hours and spread them out evenly amongst all your tasks, because they're not all equally important at all times. There's no easy formula to follow.

Instead, balance is something you'll get to define for yourself, and your definition will continually be adjusted as life changes.

Some people feel balanced when they're on the go constantly. Others don't feel balanced unless they have plenty of downtime. We each have different levels of requirements for activity, noise, alone time, free time, and so on. These are natural preferences, and there is no "right" way to feel balanced.

Think of balance as a sense of well-being that comes from spending your time on things that fit your personality and goals. When you're balanced, it feels like interruptions and setbacks can be handled, because you're not stretched too thin. Balance is knowing that most of the time, you're properly focused on things that matter, your basic needs are met, and your life is fulfilling as a whole.

When you're in balance, you don't necessarily have to focus on each of the things that are most important every day, or even every week. But you have a sense of contentment that the most valuable people, work, and obligations are your biggest priorities. You're taking care of yourself and tending to other things that matter on a regular basis, to the best of your abilities in this season of life.

Think about the core aspects of life that *you* need to attend to, in order to feel happy and fulfilled. For some people, it's easier to flip the question around: what are the core aspects of life which make you feel *unhappy* and *dissatisfied* when things get out of whack?

Write down the areas in which maintaining balance is essential to your current sense of well-being. If you don't really have to think about making time for something or check in with yourself regularly to ensure it's happening, there's no need to include it.

Avoid complicating this exercise by trying to rank your items in terms of importance. Mine are listed here in the order I originally thought of them:

1. Relationship with my husband — Was I patient, kind, and good company to be around (instead of snapping at him or being an unhelpful partner)?
2. Screens/Social media — Was I present in my own life and intentional about my time online (instead of mindlessly scrolling through posts)?
3. Work — Was I productive in getting my priorities accomplished in an appropriate amount of time (instead of procrastinating, keeping busy with unimportant tasks, or overworking)?

4. Eating — Did I eat mostly clean and healthy (instead of overindulging or eating for emotional reasons)?

5. Exercise — Did I do yoga and something to get my heart rate up (instead of spending too much time sitting down)?

I think of these as my Core 5. You might have only three or four things, or as many as six, but five seems to be a good number for many people.

If you're having trouble narrowing down your list, go back to the "fewer things better" mindset. This is not an exhaustive list of *everything* you want to balance in life, just the things that detract from your sense of happiness and fulfillment when they're off kilter. You're also ONLY writing down the things you need to constantly evaluate and work to stay balanced at.

For example, I considered adding sleep to my list here. I need to be balanced in that area, and it's extremely important to my well-being. But even though I don't sleep a full 7-8 hours every night, it is intuitive for me to go to bed earlier or sleep in later to balance things out. I rarely go more than three nights in a row without proper sleep. And, if I stay in balance with my Core 5, sleep is rarely an issue, since things like late night work and bad eating habits are what interfere with sleep.

Since I don't need to make a conscious effort to stay balanced in the area of sleep, and I already check in with myself regularly to evaluate my sleep quality, it's not on the list of core things to pay attention to. Sleep will take care of itself if I'm focused on the Core 5.

Of course, I could think of many others things I would like to stay in balance with (such as spending time with friends and having a clean and organized living space), but those things are not core to my identity. If I go too long without them, it will create unpleasant feelings. But I don't need those things to have a feeling of satisfaction and fulfillment at the end of the day. I like to make time for them as often as possible, but they are not central to my sense of well-being.

Obviously, these lists are going to be very personal. The only guiding principle for choosing your Core 5 is to avoid having more than six things. If you have more than six aspects of life that you think you need to keep in solid balance every day, you're either putting too much pressure on yourself, or you're confusing "nice to have" with "essential." See if you can figure out some things to eliminate.

How to monitor and adjust your Core 5 to live in balance

I check in with myself on my Core 5 regularly. It's not a lengthy process where I journal about it or do an elaborate reflection (though certainly you could do that, if you find it helpful).

It's just an observation process for me. I might do it as a mid-day check in, or at the end of the day when I'm brushing my teeth and getting ready for bed.

I simply think about how I feel. *Was it a satisfying day? What felt good and enjoyable today? How many of my five core areas did I attend to?*

There's usually a strong correlation between how I feel and how many of my core five areas were in balance.

On a day that felt awesome, I probably hit all five areas. No matter what else went on, if I stayed in balance with all five things, I feel happy, healthy, and like I'm winning at life. That's how I know these are my core areas that matter most to me — balance in those areas has a HUGE impact on my mood and sense of satisfaction.

If I feel a little blah when I think back on the day, I often realize that I maintained balance in three or fewer areas. But there's no judgment there. It's just a chance for observation about what choices and habits are working and which are not, so I know what to focus on the next day.

I'll remind myself,

That's okay, I did the best I could with the time and energy I had. Every moment is a fresh start, and another opportunity to pay attention to what I need.

Try to check in with yourself on a daily basis at first, and keep this exercise light. Avoid the tendency to grade or rate yourself. Just do a 30-second mental check-in when you're cleaning up after dinner, or getting ready for bed.

Notice how you feel — your mood and energy level — and how that corresponds to how many of your core areas you stayed in balance with.

Be honest with your evaluation, but keep your follow-up thoughts and self-talk positive and nurturing, as if you were speaking to a friend who was sharing their progress.

One of the nice things about evaluating balance in five core areas is that it's possible to have a good day even if you had a massive fail in one area.

If I stress-eat all day long, but got my work done and exercised, I generally don't feel too out of balance. Or if I didn't get my work done the way I'd hoped, but had a lovely day spending time with my parents and taking a break from social media, that's two huge wins. Focus on what you *are* doing to stay in balance instead of where you fell short.

Essential self-care practices to help you stay balanced

There are certain practices which I don't need daily, but do need to experience regularly in order to stay balanced with my Core 5. I don't feel like Angela if these elements aren't present in my life:

- Spending time in nature: I need to get outdoors multiple times per week
- Reading: I feel good when I am reading or listening to at least one empowering book a week
- Good conversations: I feel best when I'm talking daily with people who get me, and spending face-to-face time with friends at least every other week

I consider these to be essential self-care practices because they restore my equilibrium. They help me either stay on track or get back on track with my Core 5. When I go too long without getting out in nature, reading something inspiring, and nurturing friendships with good conversation, my Core 5 almost always falls to the wayside.

It's a predictable pattern. I start getting irritable, which creates friction in my marriage, and then I have tension instead of peace in the house. (1st core area, now out of whack.) This affects my productivity, as I'm too distracted to do my best creative work. (2nd core area messed up.) My instincts at that point are to just lay on the couch and eat junk food and scroll through social media (meaning my healthy eating, exercise, and social media habits are out the window, too).

Sometimes this can lead to anxiety or depression, and that's an easy spiral for me to fall into. Reversing course and getting back into balance with my Core 5 almost always requires me to focus on essential self-care practices.

Just a simple walk outside can clear my head and get me on track again, if I catch the problem early. If I don't, I might need a full day without work or the internet to focus on things that nourish my soul. The road back to full balance might take several days or even weeks.

When I make the conscious effort to return to my essential self-care practices, I increase the amount of willpower, motivation, and focus I have for my Core 5 and what matters most to me. These practices keep my life moving forward in the direction I want.

Since I need these self-care practices regularly (but not daily), I try to prioritize them during moments of downtime.

Instead of reaching for my phone to start the endless scroll or doing something mundane like picking up around the house, I look for something that nurtures me.

Can I read for a few minutes? Can I sit outside or take a short walk? Can I call or get on Voxer with a friend to talk about something that's interesting to me right now? Can I sit in silence and just be still for a moment?

All of those things help me thrive, and they're a better use of my time than looking for something to keep me busy. These things are essential self-care practices for me because when I do them regularly, I am able to stay in balance in my Core 5 areas.

What makes a self-care practice "essential"?

You might be ready to list out your essential self-care practices now (or maybe you already did before reading this far). You know intuitively what you need and can't wait to start implementing your ideas. Go for it!

But maybe you're not yet sure what self-care practices are necessary in your life. That's okay, too. There are downloadable templates available at FTBproject.com to help. And, you can allow your list to evolve over time as you start observing what feels good.

You might notice how the sunshine on your face and soaking up those rays tends to lift your spirit, or how being in any kind of water (a pool, jacuzzi, lake, or even a bathtub) rejuvenates you. Those might be essential self-care practices: to get outside and feel the sun for a few minutes whenever it's shining, or take a relaxing bath a couple times a week.

Maybe you love the endorphins you get from running, or the feeling of pleasure that comes from tending to beautiful, nourishing plants in your garden. Maybe playing an instrument, singing, or dancing makes you feel alive.

When your list is complete, you'll probably have around 3-6 essential self-care practices. You don't want to include ALL the things you enjoy doing or care about. We're not trying to make an exhaustive list; we're determining the essential few.

Let me give some examples of things that I did not include as essential self-care practices, and why:

Spending quality time with a pet: The mental health benefits of being around animals are well-documented, and my life wouldn't be as joyful without my cat. She and I both need time to cuddle and play together daily. But I don't need to write that down or remember to make time for her. It happens naturally, all throughout the day and evening when I'm home. So I don't need to add it as an essential self-care habit to ensure it's prioritized. It's already a habit.

Travel: Being in different environments is a powerful way to change my perspective and break through creative blockages. But travel is not an essential self-care practice because I can't just travel whenever I want to. So, if you're considering something like "walking on the beach" or "skiing" as an essential self-care practice, you need to have the location and resources to do so on a consistent basis. Otherwise, it's a self-care treat, not a habit or regular practice.

Watching my shows: One of my favorite things to do in my downtime is Netflix binging. I tune out the whole world and just get lost in a series I love. It's not on the list of essential self-care practices though, because it's not something that really nurtures my soul. It can easily devolve into something that doesn't feel good (because I overindulge) and can lead me to wreck one of my Core 5 areas (like getting my work done and eating healthy). Ultimately, if I didn't get to watch my shows, I'd be sad, but I'd adjust. It's not essential to my well-being, just a nice-to-have.

So, the things I don't have to consciously include, can't do regularly, or that aren't really soul-nurturing didn't make the cut. But being in nature, reading, and having good conversations are the essential practices. I would not feel like myself without them.

With your own list of essential self-care practices, I encourage you to write down what comes to mind intuitively first. Then go through the list and eliminate anything that:

- Is an existing habit which you already naturally make time for
- Can only be done as an infrequent treat for logistical reasons
- Potentially undermines your Core 5 (i.e. if your Core 5 includes eating healthy, then you couldn't have an essential self-care habit of eating ice cream sundaes)
- Doesn't nourish your soul (i.e. isn't one of those things that makes you say, "I feel like myself again" afterward)

Focus on identifying those essential self-care practices that enable you to stay in balance with your Core 5, so you can begin to prioritize them in your schedule.

How to build small habits and rituals of self-care into your day

The quality of your habits will determine the quality of your life. So, in addition to knowing and prioritizing your essential self-care practices, you can also look for opportunities to incorporate self-care throughout your day.

In some ways, the daily habits are even more powerful, because they give you rituals to look forward to. They can bring a moment of pleasure, presence, or wonder to everyday routines that might otherwise feel ordinary.

Additionally, self-care habits that are woven into your daily routines are easier to keep up with, because you don't have to think about them after a while. They just become part of what you do.

That's ultimately our goal with self-care, because if it's not a routine part of your life, it won't really make an impact. Most of our attempts at self-care fail because we try to do one big, nice thing for ourselves every now and then, and expect that to tide us over for weeks afterward. You get that one breakfast in bed each year or one night out with friends every six months, and hope that's somehow enough.

Self-care doesn't work that way. What you do on a regular basis is far more important than what you do occasionally. Consistency is far more important than intensity.

Your sense of balance and fulfillment is a result of the habits you form, and quality self-care is about daily choices. That's actually good news, because creating better habits is pretty simple, once you understand what works for YOU. You can start today and see results immediately.

There are countless things you can do — small, easy, free things that only take a moment or two of your time — which will increase your well-being. I've divided them into seven categories below.

You don't need to implement them all. Just notice which ones resonate most, and see if you can identify one thing you'd like to commit to starting right away.

Morning rituals

If you always wake up feeling rushed or frantic because people are making demands before your brain has kicked into gear, you might like to think about a morning ritual. This will allow you to have some time to yourself so you can mentally prepare for the day.

I never used to be a morning person, but just over a decade ago, I started getting up 15 minutes earlier than necessary, and it changed my life. I sit outside if the weather permits, have a cup of coffee, and just breathe and get my head right. Sometimes I read, listen to music, or do some stretching. But I rarely move into productivity mode until I've taken this time to center myself first. Consider even a short morning ritual for yourself that feels good and allows you to set your intentions before the hectic pace of the day begins.

Midday breaks

These self-care habits are things you do for yourself in the middle of the day so you don't feel like you're in motion from sunup to sundown. A midday break might only be a couple of minutes, and it can re-energize you for hours afterward if you pick something that works for your personality and needs.

Maybe a three-minute dance break after lunch with your students would give you a chance to have fun and let the tension go, or one minute of deep breathing or relaxation exercises after students are dismissed. Maybe you want to listen to your favorite relaxing or energizing music in the car on the way home, or sit for five minutes to have a cup of tea when you're back at your house in the afternoon.

Plan a ritual mid-day that you can look forward to, and which helps you recuperate briefly before finishing your afternoon and evening tasks.

Night rituals

You may need a night ritual if you feel like you don't get any "me time" until the whole family is in bed, and by that point, you're too exhausted to do anything for yourself.

You could shift around your tasks so that all the late night prep (setting up the coffee pot, picking out clothes for the next day, washing your face, etc.) aren't saved for right before bed. Do them right after dinner instead, so you can totally relax for the rest of the night.

Or maybe your night-time self-care will be to go to bed earlier and have 30 minutes to lay there and read or watch shows without cutting into your sleep.

Sleep habits (night-time or naps)

If you're always physically tired, make it your goal to create a self-care habit of 7 or 8 hours of sleep each night. Start with a more realistic number like 6 if needed, and work up slowly. Or, instead of forcing yourself to stay active for 18 hours straight, schedule 15 minutes into your late afternoon for lying down to rest or nap.

Reject the cultural norm that it's fine to function on a few hours of sleep every night. That is not a sustainable lifestyle, and sleep is not a special reward you only earn when you've accomplished everything on your to-do list. Sleep is integral to restoring your energy level, clearing your mind, and recovering patience and enthusiasm for everything that needs to get done. If you're sleep-deprived, choosing to address this as a measure of self-care will make a bigger difference than anything else on this list.

Mental decompression

You could set aside a specific time of day for meditation, prayer, or mindfulness practice. Or, create a ritual to help you let go of the stress of the day and transition into your home life.

One teacher I know envisions her thoughts about school as a book which she mentally closes at the end of the day and returns to the shelf, so she can choose a book on another topic after work. The school book is always there for her to reopen, and she can lose herself in it like a novel when she's back at work. But, it's a finite world which she doesn't have to be mentally immersed in all the time.

Another example is to create a curfew for social media, email, and/or school work. You could decide on none before noon on weekends, or none after 8 p.m.

These habits are crucial if you feel like you can never turn off your teacher brain and your mind is always going like a hamster on a wheel. You might even want to give yourself permission to relax by scheduling in "nothing" on your to-do list or calendar for a certain block of time.

Physical self-care

Maybe your new self-care habit will be learning to prepare healthy, delicious meals instead of always grabbing takeout, and start enjoying the rituals of cooking. Or maybe it will involve some movement that feels good to your body, such as dancing, biking, or tennis.

This is the way to go if your body is manifesting physical symptoms of stress and you need to get healthy in a way that is pleasurable.

For the purposes of self-care, think less about burning calories or getting in shape and more about responding to what your body is telling you. For instance, if you feel achy after sitting too long at the computer, build in a 15-minute walk outside. One of my physical self-care routines is stretching. I take 2-5 minute stretch breaks a few times a day, really holding the stretch and feeling my muscles lengthen. It's so much more rejuvenating than "taking a break" by checking my phone!

Creative outlets and hobbies

This is an important self-care habit to develop if you're always ensuring other people get to pursue their interests at the expense of your own. What do you love doing — maybe something you used to have time for in another season of life — which is always on the back burner now?

That might be knitting, crafting, reading, a sport, etc. Maybe you'll make a self-care habit of carving out an hour a week for your favorite hobby, or waking up 30 minutes early to write or paint each morning, or spend time paddle boarding for half an hour each week.

If there's an activity that you are passionate about, schedule time for it in your calendar as an act of self-care.

Tune in to your needs without judgment or "shoulds"

As you think about which self-care habits would be most impactful for you, be mindful of your natural tendencies when you try something new. Do you try to do everything at once and get overwhelmed? Do you start off strong and then fizzle out quickly when life gets in the way?

Try choosing just one habit to begin with, and then slowly stack more habits over time. I encourage you to begin with a habit that fits two important criteria.

First, it should be something you want to maintain for the long term. We're not going for quick fixes here. Although you can tweak the habit for your needs throughout different moods and seasons of life, you'll get the most benefit if you choose something you can stick with and make a regular part of your life for the foreseeable future.

Secondly, your self-care habit needs to have a meaningful impact on your well-being. Choose something that will make you feel happier or more rested or more productive. Don't just pick whatever sounds easiest or fun — you want this self-care habit to be something that will take a weight off your shoulders and give you a real sense of satisfaction.

It doesn't have to be big. It just has to be meaningful to you.

Self-care and balance are primarily about being in tune with your own body, thoughts, emotions, and needs. You live out balance on a daily basis by paying attention to how you feel all throughout the day, and learning more about what works for you and what doesn't.

Self-care will naturally be a part of your life once you understand the elements of your day that have a positive impact (so you can savor them and incorporate more) and the ones that have a negative impact (so you can minimize them, change your focus, or ease yourself through them with more pleasant rituals).

Don't make judgments about yourself regarding what's important in your Core 5 for staying balanced, or what you need in terms of self-care. Never ignore an area of self-care because you feel like you "shouldn't" value it as much as you do.

Also, don't pressure yourself to incorporate self-care practices that don't matter to you, simply because you feel like they "should" make the list. Self-care is about what you need to thrive, not keeping up appearances.

Accept your Core 5, essential self-care practices, and daily self-care habits the way you thought about them intuitively. No overthinking it, no second guessing, no allowing external ideas about the "right" approach to influence your thinking. Trust your intuition — what do you need in order to feel balanced at this time in your life?

The lists you brainstorm through this chapter's exercises are not meant to be exhaustive. Just because something isn't written down doesn't mean you don't care about that thing or will never prioritize it.

And, the lists are not permanent. You will find that your priorities shift during different seasons of life, and your self-care needs change over time. Everything can be adjusted later, so just focus on doing what feels right for you now.

Remind yourself that balance is never something you can achieve once and for all. The goal is to *keep actively balancing.*

You can do that by focusing on what really matters, and letting go of the rest. Return your focus to the four core beliefs you've uncovered through this book:

- You are worthy of better and change is possible for you right now.
- You set your own expectations for success in your life and teaching.
- You determine what's important and allocate your time accordingly.
- You ensure your needs are met to prevent overwhelm and exhaustion.

When you truly believe these things, you can release yourself from judgment and "shoulds."

You'll have the courage you need to do fewer things, so you can do the things that remain even better.

Afterword:
Living the fewer things better, way

To whom am I TRULY irreplaceable?

This was a question I had to answer for myself in 2009, when I chose to resign from my school district in South Florida.

My heart was telling me the next phase of my career would focus on supporting teachers, but I wasn't sure if it was time yet. I'd published my first book that year, and gotten married over the summer. My hope was to find some kind of school-based work in New York City where my husband lived. I was open to anything and ready for a change.

But the recession that year was making things difficult. In fact, the city was laying off teachers, and any kind of work in schools was extremely hard to find. I discovered my National Board Certification didn't mean much in New York, and my lack of experience within that state put me at a huge disadvantage in a competitive job market.

I couldn't see myself quitting a dependable job without having another one in place. So my husband and I made the difficult decision to continue living 1,200 miles apart.

It took six months before I was finally offered work. A consulting company hired me for a part-time instructional coaching position, and it was my dream job at that time. I'd be working with teachers in all five boroughs of the city on literacy and math instruction. I'd get to see what the different schools were like there, and make an impact on a lot of different teachers.

The catch? I had to start right away. And it was January.

The idea of leaving my students mid-year made me incredibly nervous and sad. We'd formed such a strong bond, and I adored their families. I loved my teammates. I was truly part of the school community. What would happen if I abandoned them before the school year ended? Things would never be the same for them after I left.

With great trepidation, I broke the news to my principal. She'd known this was coming for a long time, and was compassionate and kind about the situation. I offered to stay for three more weeks if needed, and help the new teacher transition in.

My principal assured me things would be fine, and she'd make the process as smooth for the kids as possible. It would be best, she thought, not to let the goodbyes drag out for too long, and to get the kids rolling with their new teacher right away.

I submitted my resignation that day, on a Monday morning.

My replacement was hired the following Wednesday. She shadowed me on Thursday. We co-taught on Friday.

And by the next Monday, I had been fully replaced.

Just days after resigning, someone else was sitting at "my" desk, using "my" computer, taking over "my" grade book, and teaching "my" kids. Just like that.

The truth was hard to swallow, but finding a suitable replacement for me was as simple as placing a job opening on the district website. Immediately, dozens of candidates who'd been surplussed from their teaching positions were in line to take my place, and I'm sure any number of them would have done a wonderful job.

My husband, however, would not have been able to replace me quite so easily as a wife (and if we'd had kids, as the mother to our children).

To my family, I was irreplaceable and indispensable.

But in my "school family," someone else had been paid to fill my shoes within a week.

It's hard not to examine what indispensability means after an experience like that. You can't help but wonder: Who in your life finds you truly irreplaceable? Who are the people that deserve your greatest loyalty?

I feel confident that my decision was the right one. I moved on from that job literally and figuratively, and I'm able to prioritize the work I do currently (including writing this book) as a result of the choice I made that year.

That group of students has now graduated from high school and they're off living their lives, too. I doubt that any of them are sitting in a therapist's chair talking about how a third grade teacher they thought they'd have for ten months was actually only there for six months and they've never been able to recover emotionally or academically from that loss.

I don't mean to sound flippant. A mid-year transition is far from ideal, and any upheaval can be detrimental to kids. I know my presence was missed, especially at first.

But we've all seen awesome teachers leave our schools and we know things carry on without them. The person quickly becomes a memory:

"Aw, I miss going by her door to see her" or "Remember what a great job she did with the science fair? Sure wish she was here to help with that again this year."

And yet the science fair goes on, and so does the learning in that classroom. Things are different, but somehow the school does NOT fall apart, and a new normal is created more quickly than we could have ever imagined.

No matter how many well-intentioned people assure you things wouldn't be the same without you, the truth is that the school will find someone else to take your place.

That doesn't mean you're unimportant.

It means you don't have to pressure yourself to hold everything together. If they could find a way to make things work with someone who's not you, surely they can find a way when you're still there but simply stepping back a bit on your commitments.

The fact that you're not irreplaceable also means you're not stuck. No job has to be forever. You can find another workplace where you get more support, appreciation, resources, or compensation.

Remember, winners quit all the time: they just quit the right things at the right time. This is your career, and it's your life. You can take charge of it.

My hope is that you would use this book as a springboard to help you find your path in making education a more fulfilling and sustainable career if that's what you choose. I want you to feel empowered to exercise your agency: to leave your school when you need to, and to stay and create change when that's the right course of action.

I also hope this book will broaden the scope of our discussions about burnout, and bring more mainstream awareness to the conversations that are already happening on the margins and behind closed doors.

What I've shared with you here is not meant to be a comprehensive answer to the systemic problems in education. Parallel solutions are needed, and there are many other tactics required to address the ways teachers are exploited and schools are under-resourced.

Many of those solutions go beyond what an individual educator can do. I think it would be unfair for me to insist you spend your evenings and weekends organizing protests and calling your congressional reps. It's powerful if you choose to do that, but as someone who's not in the classroom myself, it's inappropriate for me to imply that burden is yours to carry.

I believe it's up to the rest of us to do the heavy lifting when it comes to institutional change.

Thought leaders and education influencers need to speak up about what's right, and not just regurgitate the safe messages that brands and districts are paying them to say.

Administrators, superintendents, and other school leaders need to facilitate these conversations within their districts, and do their part to shift school norms and teacher expectations.

Communities and families need to stand up for their children and teachers, and fight against the excessive accountability measures and standardization of our schools.

We need to be in this struggle together, and each play our part.

And my personal contribution right now is based in speaking truth and living it out to create grassroots change.

I believe that you and I have the ability to make an impact on the world through the things we focus our time and energy on.

I believe in the power of each of us as individuals to stand up for what's right and interrupt patterns that are harmful.

I believe that freeing ourselves from beliefs and expectations which don't serve us well is one of the most powerful ways to create change.

The way we show up in the world has a tremendous impact on those around us. Our actions can inspire and influence others. We can create a ripple effect.

When we live as our true, essential selves — whole and healthy and free — we have the courage that is needed to carve out a different path. We can step into our natural role as leaders, and embody the change we want to see in our schools and communities.

These steps to devote our best time and energy to the things that matter most require thinking outside the box and disrupting the status quo.

And we can do that, together.

It's not going to be easy. It's going to be worth it.

How to stay connected and get more resources

I want this book to be just the beginning of your renewed quest to do fewer things better. If you are truly committed to maintaining the courage to focus on what matters most, you'll get the best results if you're part of a community of educators who will support you in that journey. You don't have to figure this out alone, or be the only teacher you know who's committed to questioning norms.

Start by downloading the Fewer Things Better Project. This is a free mini-course with a printable workbook to help you implement all the ideas you've read.

The Fewer Things Better Project will help you strategically implement what you learned through the book and reflect on how you want to be spending your time. You'll be able to think through what balance looks like in your current season of life, and define your legacy, daily priorities, and self-care needs.

It will also help you develop confidence in your teaching style, and give you the opportunity to reflect on what's working (and what to cut back on). If you're feeling empowered by this book and want to articulate a clear vision for what fewer things better will look like in your life, you'll definitely want to participate in the project.

You might also consider joining the 40 Hour Teacher Workweek Club. This is a yearlong professional development program I created to offer step-by-step support in focusing on what matters most. It's a good option if you are a K-12 teacher and want tactical advice and strategies for streamlining every aspect of your work, from lesson planning to grading to technology to parent communication.

You'll get hundreds of dollars' worth of forms and templates, and have a community of other like-minded teachers and mentors to encourage you and hold you accountable. The club requires a one-time financial investment up front, and is well worth it for teachers who are serious about creating permanent change in how their time is used.

If you're tired of reinventing the wheel, the club will take out the guesswork of simplifying and give you a proven system. As of 2019, the 40 Hour Teacher Workweek Club has been used in more than 25,000 schools, and I'm so proud of the impact it's made for teachers who want a sustainable approach to doing the work they love for years to come.

Here are some other ways to stay connected with me and get new ideas and resources for doing fewer things better:

- Subscribe to my Truth for Teachers podcast for inspiring audio messages
- Sign up for weekly encouragement and strategies via email
- Follow me on Instagram, Twitter, or Facebook
- Inquire about having me speak or conduct PD at your school

I would love for you to reach out via social media or email and introduce yourself. There's nothing that inspires my work more than hearing from teachers who are determined to create change and think outside the box. You've heard my story — now it's time to tell yours!

Go to FewerThingsBetterBook.com to access all the resources and contact methods listed here.

Acknowledgments

I want to extend a huge show of gratitude toward all the people who helped make this book possible, in particular:

To Eliza Geswein, who created the awesome illustrations inside this book and all of the original artwork for the book's promotional materials. Thank you for working on a tight deadline, and for creating such beautiful illustrations for my favorite excerpts and quotes.

To Monica Macaraeg, who proofread the book and did a ton of hard work behind the scenes. Thank you for your longstanding commitment as a part of my team, and for being willing to tackle anything that needs to be done to bring my resources to more teachers.

To Kali Engelbert, who offered editorial guidance and provided input on every aspect of publication. Thank you for your attention to detail, and unfailing focus on the best interests of the company as well as the teachers we serve. Your deep desire to ensure everything is done with excellence is so appreciated.

To Amber Teamann, who was the first beta reader for this book. Thank you for your never-ending enthusiasm for my work, as well as your willingness to be candid and honest in all things.

To Jennifer Gonzalez, whose daily moral support and professional advice have become priceless to me. I respect your opinion and our friendship so much, and am grateful for the time you have invested in us.

To my mastermind friends (including John Spencer, AJ Juliani, Chris Kesler, and Jen Bengel), who would be zillionaires if they had a dollar for every time I've said, "So I have this idea and I want your opinion." Thank you for helping me think through the logistics of all my many plans, offering advice from the deep wellspring of your experience, and inspiring me to think big.

To my parents, who believed I was a teacher and a writer before I did. Thank you for seeing these gifts in me, and doing everything you could to provide me with the education and resources I needed to meet my goals.

To my husband, who has been through the ups and downs of the publishing process with me five times now. Thank you for giving me the space to create and get lost in my own inner world. Thank you for not only allowing me to evolve and change as a person throughout our marriage, but for growing right alongside me. Thank you for encouraging me to be myself, trust myself, and follow my own intuition. I have more courage to focus on what matters because you have supported me in discovering that path, and you're committed to living it out with me.

To all the teachers who have believed in my mission, some of whom have been on this journey since 2003 when I created my first website. Thank you for sticking with me through all the changes (in education, the online space, and in the focus of my work). Nothing that I create would have meaning if you didn't utilize it and share it. Your kind words renew my enthusiasm, and keep me going when I feel stuck or overwhelmed. Thank you for supporting me and making it possible for me to do the work I love: helping *you* do the work you love.

CPSIA information can be obtained
at www.ICGtesting.com
Printed in the USA
BVHW052029281021
620215BV00008B/95

9 780982 312742